WE MEAN BUSINESS

An elementary course in business English

Students' Book

Susan Norman
with Eleanor Melville

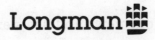

Contents

Contents

Contents

iv

Unit One
A visitor to BOS

Fred McLean is introducing a visitor to some of the BOS staff.

Exercise 1

1. What is the visitor's name?
2. Where does the visitor come from?
3. Does George know Mary?
4. What does Paul Johnson do?
5. Does George know Paul?

1

Brighter Office Supplies Ltd (BOS) is a company which makes and sells office equipment. The head office is in Harlow in Essex. Look at this page from the BOS magazine.

Some of the BOS staff at Harlow head office
Our motto is
`We Mean Business`

Fred McLean

Luisa Middle (Mrs)

Simon Young

Sheila Baker (Mrs)

Howard Spencer

Mary Mackie (Miss)

Paul Johnson

Joy Bradley (Miss)

Exercise 2   *Are they married?*

In pairs, talk about the BOS staff, like this:

A: *Is Luisa married?*   B: *Yes. She's Mrs Middle.*
A: *Is Mary . . .?*   B: *No. She's Miss Mackie.*
A: *. . . Fred . . .?*   B: *I don't know.*

NB	Titles		*Woman*		*Man*
	married:	Mrs Middle	Ms Middle		Mr McLean
	single:	Miss Mackie	Ms Mackie		

2

What do they do?

Exercise 3

 Listen to the tape. The editor of the BOS magazine is talking to Howard Spencer. Here are the names of some of the BOS staff and a list of jobs. Put the right name with the right job, like this: 1 – b

Names		*Jobs*	
1	Fred McLean	a	a sales manager
2	Luisa Middle	b	a managing director
3	Simon Young	c	a secretary
4	Sheila Baker	d	a sales representative
5	Mary Mackie	e	a receptionist
6	Paul Johnson	f	a personnel manager
7	Joy Bradley	g	a personal secretary
8	Howard Spencer	h	a sales assistant

Exercise 4

Write sentences about the BOS staff, like this:

1 *Fred McLean is a managing director.*
2 *Luisa Middle is . . .*

Exercise 5

In pairs, talk about what people do at BOS, like this:
A: *What does Fred do?* B: *He's a managing director.*
A: *What does Luisa do?* B: *She's . . .*

NB For a man we say *he*, for a woman we say *she*.
We write *he is* and *she is*, but we say *he's* and *she's*. In this book we write *he's*, *she's* etc for a speaking exercise.

Exercise 6

In pairs, talk about the BOS staff like this:

A: *Is Luisa a receptionist?*   B: *Yes she is.*
A: *Is Paul a secretary?*   B: *No he isn't.*
A: *Is Mary . . .?*

NB   With short answers we say *Yes she is.* We do not say *Yes she's.*

Laboratory drill
P: Is Luisa a receptionist?   R: *Yes she is.*
P: Is Paul a secretary?   R: *No he isn't.*

Exercise 7   *Organisation chart*

Here is part of the BOS organisation chart:

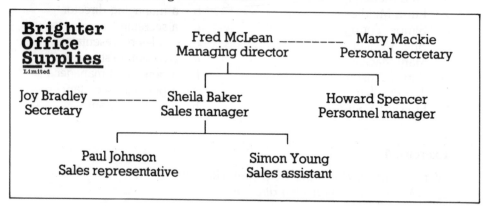

In pairs, use these notes to talk about the BOS staff, like this:
Mary – boss
A: *Who is Mary's boss?*   B: *Fred*

NB   Your *boss* is the person you work for. Here *'s* shows the relationship between people. It does not mean *is*.

1 Mary – boss
2 Paul – boss
3 Sheila – boss
4 Sheila – assistant

5 Fred – personal secretary
6 Simon – boss
7 Sheila – secretary
8 Howard – boss

Laboratory drill A
P: Who's Mary's boss?   R: *Fred*

Laboratory drill B
P: Mary – boss   R: *Who's Mary's boss?*

Exercise 8   *Introducing people*

Look at this dialogue. George and Mary do not know each other.
A: *George, this is Mary. Mary, this is George.*
GEORGE: *Pleased to meet you, Mary.*
MARY: *How do you do.*

Go round the class and introduce people in the same way.

Exercise 9   *Greeting people*

Look at this dialogue. These two people know each other.
PAUL: *Hello, George. It's good to see you again.*
GEORGE: *Hello, Paul. How are you?*
PAUL: *Very well thank you. And you?*
GEORGE: *Fine thanks.*

Go round the class and greet people you know in the same way.

Laboratory drill A
Say George's part in the dialogue.

Laboratory drill B
Say Paul's part in the dialogue.

Exercise 10   *Registering at a hotel*

Two guests are registering at a hotel in Harlow. The receptionist is asking them for information. Fill in two registration forms like this, with the information on the tape.

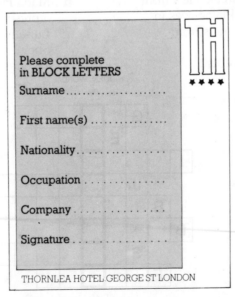

Please complete
in BLOCK LETTERS

Surname......................

First name(s) ....

Nationality.................

Occupation ....

Company ....

Signature ....

THORNLEA HOTEL GEORGE ST LONDON

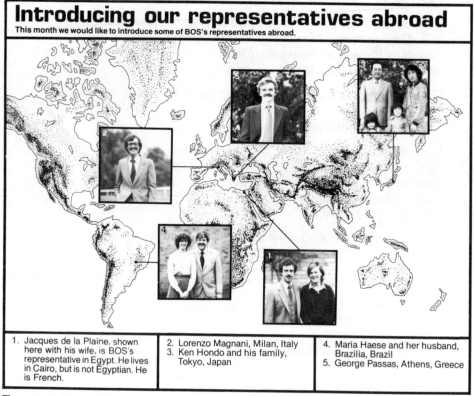

Introducing our representatives abroad

This month we would like to introduce some of BOS's representatives abroad.

1. Jacques de la Plaine, shown here with his wife, is BOS's representative in Egypt. He lives in Cairo, but is not Egyptian. He is French.

2. Lorenzo Magnani, Milan, Italy
3. Ken Hondo and his family, Tokyo, Japan

4. Maria Haese and her husband, Brazilia, Brazil
5. George Passas, Athens, Greece

Exercise 11 *Word puzzle*

Use the clues to fill in a copy of this word puzzle and find the hidden word. All the answers are countries or nationalities.

Clues

1 Mr Passas is Greek. He's from . . .
2 Jacques de la Plaine lives in . . .
3 Lorenzo Magnani is from . . .
4 Ken Hondo is . . .
5 Howard Spencer is . . .

6 Maria Haese is the BOS representative in . . .
7 Luisa Middle is from Spain. She's . . .
8 Jacques de la Plaine is . . .

HIDDEN WORD

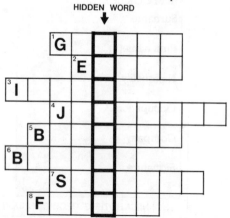

— **Exercise 12** *Personal information*

Talk about the BOS representatives, like this:

A: *What's his first name?*	B: *Jacques.*
A: *What's his surname?*	B: *de la Plaine.*
A: *What's his nationality?*	B: *He's French*
or A: *Where is he from?*	B: *France.*
A: *What does he do?*	B: *He's BOS's representative in Egypt.*
A: *Is he married?*	B: *Yes he is.*

NB Maria Haese: What's *her* first name? Where's *she* from?

Laboratory drill A
P: What's his first name?   R: *What's her first name?*

Laboratory drill B
P: What's his first name?   R: *What's your first name?*

Exercise 13 *Questionnaire*

	First name	Surname	Occupation	Nationality	Marital status
eg	Luisa	Middle	receptionist	Spanish	married
YOU					

Fill in the second line of a questionnaire like this with real or imaginary facts
about you. Go round the class and talk to five different people. Ask them
questions from the questionnaire and fill in their answers.

The first question you ask is: *What's your first name?*
Perhaps you will not hear an answer. Say: *Can you say that again please?*
Or you can ask them to spell a difficult word: *Can you spell that please?*

Language notes

The alphabet

A a – B b – C c – D d – E e – F f – G g – H h – I i – J j – K k – L l – M m –
N n – O o – P p – Q q – R r – S s – T t – U u – V v – W w – X x – Y y – Z z

Vowels: a e i o u (y)
Consonants: b c d f g h j k l m n p q r s t v w x (y) z

To be (present tense)

Positive		*Negative*	
(written)	(spoken)	(written)	(spoken)
I am	I'm	I am not	I'm not
you are	you're	you are not	you're not/you aren't
he is	he's	he is not	he's not/he isn't
she is	she's	she is not	she's not/she isn't
it is	it's	it is not	it's not/it isn't
we are	we're	we are not	we're not/we aren't
they are	they're	they are not	they're not/they aren't

Question	*Short answer*
Am I . . .?	Yes I am. No I'm not.
Are you . . .?	Yes you are. No you're not./No you aren't.
Is he . . .?	Yes he is. No he's not./No he isn't.
Is she . . .?	Yes she is. No she's not./No she isn't.
Is it . . .?	Yes it is. No it's not./No it isn't.
Are we . . .?	Yes we are. No we're not./No we aren't.
Are they . . .?	Yes they are. No they're not./No they aren't.

Question words

What is your name?	(What's)
Where is he from?	(Where's)
Who is Mary's boss?	(Who's)

Possessive pronouns

My Your His Her Its	name is . . .	Our Your Their	names are . . .

Genitive ('s) = belonging to

The book belonging to Mary – Mary's book
The staff of BOS – BOS's (or BOS') staff
The book belonging to the assistant – the assistant's book

Unit Two
A newcomer

Anne Bell is Sheila Baker's new secretary. She is starting work today. Joy Bradley is Sheila's former secretary. Joy is showing Anne the office.

1 Well, this is the office. And this is Simon Young. Simon and I share the office.

2 Simon, this is Anne.

Hello, Anne. Nice to meet you. Welcome to BOS.

Thank you.

3 This is your desk and these are your telephones.

4 This is the internal phone . . .

and that's the external phone.

5 Those are your shelves.

6 The coffee pot's on the bottom shelf.

Exercise 14

1 Who does Joy share the office with?
2 How many telephones has Anne got?
3 Where are the telephones?
4 Where is the coffee pot?

9

Exercise 15   *Office furniture*

Look at these pictures. Then look at the pictures on page 2 again.

1 notice board	2 desk	3 telephone	4 chair

5 typewriter	6 wastepaper bin	7 graph	8 filing cabinet

In pairs, talk about the pictures like this:

Picture 1   A: *What's this?*   B: *It's a notice board*
              A: *Is it Fred's notice board?* B: *Yes it is.*

Picture 2   A: *What's . . .?*   B: *It's a . . .*
              A: *Is it Sheila's desk?*   B: *No it isn't. It's Simon's desk.*

Laboratory drill A
P: Picture 1. What's this?   R: *It's a notice board.*

Laboratory drill B
P: Picture 1. Is it Fred's notice board?   R: *Yes it is.*
P: Picture 2. Is it Sheila's desk?   R: *No it isn't. It's Simon's desk.*

Exercise 16   *Office equipment*

In pairs, talk about these pictures, like this:
A: *What's this? Is it a desk or a table?*   B: *It's a desk.*

1 desk/table	2 wastepaper bin/chair	3 photocopier/telephone

4 filing cabinet/in-tray	5 typewriter/calculator	6 letter/book

7 drawer/shelf	8 pot plant/coffee pot	9 notice board/graph
		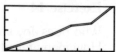

Laboratory drill A
P: Picture 1. What's this? Is it a desk or a   R: *It's a desk.*
   table?

Laboratory drill B
P: Picture 1. Desk or table   R: *What's this? Is it a desk or a table?*

Exercise 17   *Mixed-up words*

The letters of these words are in the wrong order. They are all things you find in an office. What are they? eg YART = tray

1	SAWPREPATE NIB	2	SKED	3	FEHLS
4	WARDER	5	NICTOE BRODA	6	PETELNHOE
7	NILFIG BATINEC	8	SKOBO	9	OCOTPOPHRIE

Exercise 18   *Hidden word puzzle*

Learn the prepositions on page 17. Use the clues to help you fill in a copy of this puzzle and find the hidden word. The answers are all prepositions.

Clues Where's x in these clues?

1   It's . . . z.
2&3 It's . . . . . . y.
4   It's . . . w.
5   It's to the . . . of y.

6   It's . . . the table.
7   It's . . . the wastepaper bin.

HIDDEN WORD

Write a sentence using the hidden word.

Exercise 19   *Numbers*

Learn the cardinal numbers from 1 to 20 (see note on page 17). Listen to the tape. Write down the number you hear in each sentence. Write down the number only. There are fifteen (15) sentences. eg Sentence 1: *12*

Now go back and spell each number, like this: Sentence 1: 12 – *twelve*

Exercise 20 *Showing someone where things are*

You are showing Anne things in the office. Make twelve (12) sentences about these pictures using the notes, like this:

1 *This is your desk.*   2 *These are . . .*
7 *That's the notice board.*   8 *Those are . . .*

1	2	3	4	5	6

This is	4 your in-tray
	1 your desk
	6 your typewriter

These are	2 your trays
	5 your drawers
	3 your telephones

7	8	9	10	11	12

That's	12 the photocopier
	9 the coffee pot
	7 the notice board

Those are	11 the filing cabinets
	10 the shelves
	8 the books

Laboratory drill
P: Picture 1. What's this?   R: *This is your desk.*
P: Picture 2. What are these?   R: *These are your trays.*
P: Picture 7. What's that?   R: *That's the notice board.*
P: Picture 8. What are those?   R: *Those are the books.*

Exercise 21 *Anne's office*

Look at this picture of Anne and Simon's office. Anne's desk is on the left and Simon's desk is on the right.

Are these sentences *true* or *false*? Correct the false sentences, like this:

1 There are two telephones on Anne's desk. – *True*
2 There are three typewriters in the room. – *False. There are two typewriters in the room.*

3 There is a photocopier on the table.
4 There is a pot plant in a filing cabinet.
5 The notice board is next to the shelves.
6 The graph is between the notice board and the shelves.
7 There is a book on the bottom shelf.
8 There are ten filing cabinets.
9 The wastepaper bin is under the table.
10 The coffee pot is on the top shelf.
11 There are three trays on the table.
12 There is a calculator on Anne's desk.
13 The graph is on the wall above the table.
14 The notice board is under Simon's desk.

Exercise 22 *Where is it?*

In pairs, describe and guess where something is in Anne's office, like this:

A: *It's on the wall above the table.*   B: *Is it the notice board?*
A: *No. It's between the shelves and*   B: *Is it the graph?*
     the notice board.
A: *Yes it is.*

Business letter format

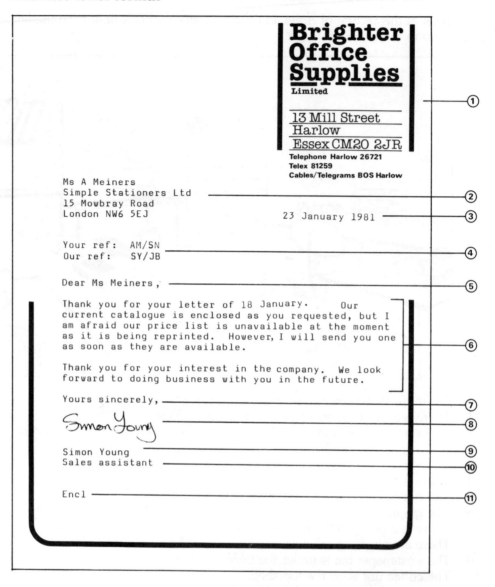

Brighter Office Supplies Limited ── ①

13 Mill Street
Harlow
Essex CM20 2JR
Telephone Harlow 26721
Telex 81259
Cables/Telegrams BOS Harlow

Ms A Meiners
Simple Stationers Ltd ──────── ②
15 Mowbray Road
London NW6 5EJ
                                23 January 1981 ──── ③

Your ref: AM/SN ──────────── ④
Our ref: SY/JB

Dear Ms Meiners, ──────────── ⑤

Thank you for your letter of 18 January.   Our
current catalogue is enclosed as you requested, but I
am afraid our price list is unavailable at the moment
as it is being reprinted. However, I will send you one
as soon as they are available. ── ⑥

Thank you for your interest in the company. We look
forward to doing business with you in the future.

Yours sincerely, ──────────── ⑦

Simon Young ──────────── ⑧

Simon Young ──────────── ⑨
Sales assistant ──────────── ⑩

Encl ──────────── ⑪

NB 2	*Reader's name and address*	Simple Stationers 15 Mowbray Road London NW6 5EJ	Sales manager Simple Stationers 15 Mowbray Road London NW6 5EJ	Ms A Meiners Simple Stationers 15 Mowbray Road London NW6 5EJ
5	*Opening salutation*	Dear Sirs,	Dear Sir, Dear Sir or Madam,	Dear Ms Meiners,
7	*Closing salutation*	Yours faithfully,	Yours faithfully,	Yours sincerely,

You don't know the reader's name   *You know the reader's name*

Exercise 23

 Look at the business letter and listen to the tape. A business school teacher is explaining the parts of a business letter to a student. Make a list of the numbers and the correct parts of the letter, like this: 1 – *letterhead*

These are the parts of the letter:
body of the letter/letterhead/writer's name/date/references/enclosures/ signature/opening salutation/closing salutation/writer's position in the company/reader's name and address

Exercise 24

In pairs, talk about the parts of a letter, like this:

A: *Where's the signature?*   B: *It's below the closing salutation.*
A: *Where's the . . .?*   B: *It's at the top of the letter.*

Telephoning

These are the room numbers and telephone numbers of the BOS staff:

```
BOS office number: Harlow 26721 (10 lines)
```

Name	Room no.	Ext. no.	Home no.
Sheila Baker	103	62	739 2202
Joy Bradley (Anne Bell)	102	67	627 5183 (123 9876)
Paul Johnson	101	58	459 8116
Mary Mackie	207	55	486 7031
Fred McLean	205	57	–
Luisa Middle	reception	81	–
Howard Spencer	206	60	242 7951
Simon Young	102	70	328 6659

Exercise 25

In pairs, talk about the numbers, like this:

A: *What's Sheila's room number?*   B: *One – oh – three*
A: *What's her extension number?*   B: *Sixty-two*
A: *What's her home number?*   B: *Seven – three – nine – double two – oh – two*

Laboratory drill A P: What's Sheila's room number?	R: *One – oh – three*
Laboratory drill B P: What's Sheila's extension number?	R: *Sixty-two*
Laboratory drill C P: What's Sheila's home number?	R: *Seven–three–nine–double two–oh–two*

Exercise 26

In pairs, pretend you are the BOS staff and answer the phone, like this:

SHEILA: (answers phone) *739 2202.*
CALLER: *Hello. Is that Sheila?*
SHEILA: *Yes it is.*
CALLER: *Oh. Hello, Sheila. This is David.*

Laboratory drill A
Say the caller's part in the dialogue.

Laboratory drill B
Say Sheila's part in the dialogue.

Exercise 27

In pairs, talk on the phone, like this:

SIMON: (answers phone) *328-6659.*
CALLER: *Hello. Is that Paul?*
SIMON: *No. This is 328-6659.*
CALLER: *Sorry. Wrong number.*

Laboratory drill A
Say the caller's part in the dialogue.

Laboratory drill B
Say Simon's part in the dialogue.

Exercise 28

In pairs, talk on the phone, like this:

SWITCHBOARD: *Number please.*
CALLER: *459 8116 please.*
SWITCHBOARD: *Just a moment . . . You're through.*
CALLER: *Hello. Is that Paul?*

Laboratory drill A
Say the caller's part in the dialogue.

Laboratory drill B
Say the switchboard girl's part in the dialogue.

Language notes

Some prepositions

It's *to the left of* the desk.

It's *next to* the desk.

It's *in* the corner.

It's *on* the desk.

It's *behind* the telephone.

1 at the top
2 on the left
3 on the right } of the
4 at the bottom   picture
5 in the middle

It's *on* the wall.

It's *above* the desk.

It's *next to* the desk.

It's *to the right of* the desk.

It's *on* the desk.

It's *in front of* the plant.

It's *under* the desk.

It's *below* the picture.

It's *between* the filing cabinet and the chair.

It's *in* the drawer.

Cardinal numbers

0	oh/zero/nought	10	ten	20	twenty
1	one	11	eleven	31	thirty-one
2	two	12	twelve	42	forty-two
3	three	13	thirteen	53	fifty-three
4	four	14	fourteen	64	sixty-four
5	five	15	fifteen	75	seventy-five
6	six	16	sixteen	86	eighty-six
7	seven	17	seventeen	97	ninety-seven
8	eight	18	eighteen	100	a hundred, one hundred
9	nine	19	nineteen	500	five hundred (*not* five hundreds)*

638   six hundred and thirty-eight
1,000   a thousand, one thousand
10,000   ten thousand (*not* ten thousands)*
100,000   a hundred thousand
1,000,000   a million,* one million
1,000,000,000   a thousand million (UK); a billion (US)
1,000,000,000,000   a billion* (UK)
Hundred, thousand, million and *billion* always remain in the singular in numbers

Unit Three
The BOS building

Joy and Anne are in Anne's new office on the first floor, Room 102. Joy is showing Anne around the BOS building.

Exercise 29

1 Where is the medical room?
2 Is Paul in his office?

3 What is Fred McLean doing today?
4 Who is reading a magazine?

What are they doing now?

Exercise 30

 Look at these pictures and the notes and listen to the tape. Two people are talking about what the BOS staff are doing. It is exactly midday. Write each picture number with the correct note, like this: 1 – b

1 Luisa   2 Anne   3 Howard   4 Joy   5 Fred

6 Simon   7 Mary   8 Helen   9 Paul

Notes

9 a have lunch   5 d visit a customer   2 g type a letter 2

^ b welcome a visitor 4 e take shorthand .steno 7 h send a telex

8 c read a magazine 3 f interview someone 6 i talk on the phone

Exercise 31

In pairs, use your notes from Exercise 30 to talk about what the people at BOS are doing now, like this:

A: *What's Luisa doing?*   B: *She's welcoming a visitor.*

NB You use the present progressive tense for things people are doing now (see note on page 25).

Laboratory drill
P: What's Luisa doing?   R: *She's welcoming a visitor.*

Exercise 32

In pairs, talk about what the people at BOS are doing, like this:

A: *Is Luisa welcoming a visitor?*   B: *Yes she is.*
A: *Are Simon and Joy having lunch?* B: *No they're not. Simon's . . . and Joy's . . .*

Laboratory drill
P: Is Luisa welcoming a visitor?   R: *Yes she is.*
P: Are Simon and Joy having lunch? R: *No they're not.*

Unit 3

Exercise 33 *Telephoning*

In pairs, ask to speak to people at BOS on the phone and say what they are doing, like this:

A: *Can I speak to Howard Spencer please?*
B: *I'm afraid not. He's interviewing someone.*

je crainds que non

Ask to speak to: 1 Howard Spencer 4 Simon Young
2 Joy Bradley 5 Paul Johnson
3 Fred McLean

Laboratory drill A
P: Can I speak to Howard Spencer please?   R: *I'm afraid not. He's interviewing someone.*

Laboratory drill B
P: Fred McLean   R: *Can I speak to Fred McLean please?*

Exercise 34 *Present progressive*

Write sentences in the present progressive tense about what people are doing now, like this:

The managers (have) a meeting. – The managers are having a meeting.

NB Be careful of the spelling of the verbs (see page 25 for spelling rules).

1 He (think). *is thinking*
2 They (visit) customers. *are visiting*
3 We (eat) our lunch. *are eating*
4 Luisa (greet) a visitor. *is greeting*
5 Mary (take) shorthand. *is taking*
6 You (have) lunch. *are having*
7 You (write) a letter. *are writing*
8 Sheila (interview) someone. *is interviewing*
9 I (speak) on the phone. *I'm speaking*
10 Helen (sit) in her office. *is sitting*
11 The salesman (sell) stationery. *is selling*
12 He (read) a report. *is reading*
13 I (put) these books on the table. *I'm putting*
14 She (get) on the bus. *is getting*

Exercise 35 *Ordinal numbers*

Learn the ordinal numbers from *1st* to *20th* (see page 24).
Listen to the tape. There are ten sentences. Write down the ordinal number you hear in each sentence, like this: Sentence 1: *7th*

Then write the correct spelling of each ordinal number, like this:
Sentence 1: *7th – seventh*

Which floor?

Exercise 36

Look at this board. It is on the ground floor of the BOS building in Harlow.
There are other companies in the building too. Follow the lines and write
the number of the floor each company is on a copy of the board.

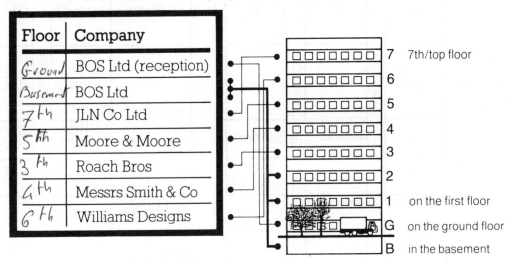

Floor	Company
Ground	BOS Ltd (reception)
Basement	BOS Ltd
7th	JLN Co Ltd
5th	Moore & Moore
3th	Roach Bros
4th	Messrs Smith & Co
6th	Williams Designs

7 7th/top floor
6
5
4
3
2
1 on the first floor
G on the ground floor
B in the basement

Exercise 37

In pairs, talk about where the companies are, like this:
A: *Which floor is Roach Bros on?*   B: *It's on the . . . floor.*
A: *Which company is on the first floor?*   B: *BOS Ltd.*

Laboratory drill A
P: Which floor is Roach Brothers on?   R: *It's on the third floor.*

Laboratory drill B
P: Seventh   R: *Which company is on the seventh floor?*

Exercise 38   *Commands*

In pairs, use the words below to make sentences telling people to do things. One
person makes a command, the other person obeys the command, like this:
A says *Stand up* – B stands up.
B says *Touch a book* – A touches a book.

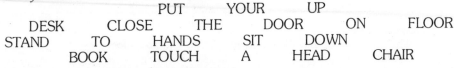

PUT   YOUR   UP
DESK   CLOSE   THE   DOOR   ON   FLOOR
STAND   TO   HANDS   SIT   DOWN
BOOK   TOUCH   A   HEAD   CHAIR

NB   See note on the imperative on page 25.

Unit 3

The BOS building

This is the layout of the basement, the ground floor and the first floor of the BOS building. The layout of floors 2 to 7 is the same as the first floor.

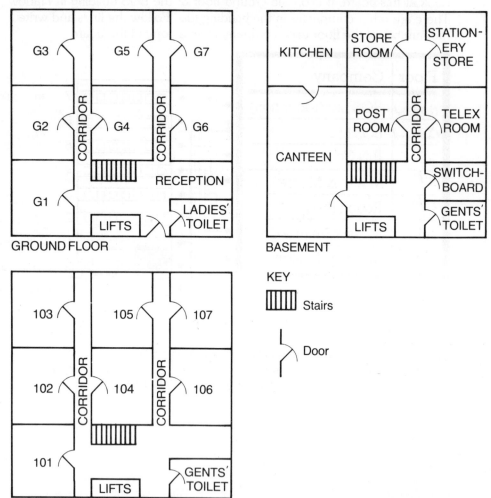

GROUND FLOOR

BASEMENT

KEY

▓▓▓▓ Stairs

⌐⌐ Door

FIRST FLOOR   (all other floors are the same but Ladies' and Gents' toilets are on alternate floors)

Exercise 39

In pairs, talk about the BOS building using these words:
next to/opposite/between/above/below
Like this:
A: *Where's the post room?*   B: *It's next to the store room, opposite the telex room and below room G4.*

Laboratory drill
P: Which room is opposite the stationery store?   R: *The store room*

22

Exercise 40

You are in reception. In pairs, ask for and give directions in the BOS building, like this.

A: *Excuse me. Where's the canteen please?*
B: *It's downstairs in the basement.*
A: *Is it on the right or on the left?*
B: *Come out of the lift and it's on the left.*

Laboratory drill
P: The canteen   R: *Excuse me. Where's the canteen please?*

 Exercise 41

In pairs, ask for and give directions in the BOS building, like this:

A: *Excuse me. Where's room 405 please?*
B: *Come out of the lift on the fourth floor and take the corridor on the right. Room 405 is on the left.*
A: *Thank you.*
B: *You're welcome.*

Laboratory drill
P: Come out of the lift on the fourth floor and take the corridor on the right. It's on the right.
R: *Room 406 or 407*

Exercise 42   Word puzzle

Use the clues to help you fill in a copy of this word puzzle.

Clues

This ⌐ means a (1).
Reception is (11) the (2) floor.
(3) is the opposite of *upstairs*.
(6) is the (7) of *down*.
Come (5) (4) the (9).
The canteen is (8) the (10).
Room 101 is on the first (12).

Exercise 43   *A memorandum*

Look at the memo from Howard Spencer.

MEMORANDUM

Brighter Office Supplies
Limited

TO: All staff
FROM: Howard Spencer, Personnel department
DATE: 23 November 1981
Subject: Staff welfare

I am available to see staff on Monday and Wednesday between
9.30 and 11.30am in my office. I can also see staff by
appointment.

My office is room 206 on the second floor. Come out of the
lift and take the corridor on the right. Room 206 is on the
right.

Write a similar memo to the staff from the company nurse, Jane Seymour. It is about the medical room hours. Say what time the nurse is available and where the medical room is. Look at the plan on page 22 to see where room 203 is.

This is your information:
Medical room hours: Tuesday and Thursday, 10.30 – 3.30 or by appointment
Medical room: Room 203

Language notes

Ordinal numbers

1st	first	10th	tenth
2nd	second	11th	eleventh
3rd	third	12th	twelfth
4th	fourth	13th	thirteenth
5th	fifth	20th	twentieth
6th	sixth	31st	thirty-first
7th	seventh	42nd	forty-second
8th	eighth	53rd	fifty-third
9th	ninth	64th	sixty-fourth

100th   a hundredth
1,000th   a thousandth
Other ordinal numbers are made by adding *-th* to the cardinal numbers unless they end in -1, -2 or -3.

Present progressive tense

(also called the present continuous tense)

We use the present progressive to talk about things which are happening now.

to be + verb + ing

Positive

I am typing	(I'm typing)
you are eating	(you're)
s/he is going	(he's/she's)
we are writing	(we're)
they are meeting	(they're)

Negative

I am not typing (I'm not)
you are not eating (you're not/you aren't)
he is not going (he's not/he isn't)
we are not writing (we're not/we aren't)
they are not meeting (they're not/they aren't)

Question

Am I typing?
Is she talking?

Short answer

Yes I am.	No I'm not.
Yes she is.	No she's not./No she isn't.

Spelling

go + ing	= going	typ~~e~~ + ing	= typing
talk + ing	= talking	writ~~e~~ + ing	= writing

NB

short vowel + one consonant
begin + n + ing = beginning
get + t + ing = getting

but long vowel + one consonant
read + ing = reading
feel + ing = feeling
tear + ing = tearing

See also the list of irregular verbs on page 139.

Question words

What are you eating?
Where is he going? (Where's)
Who's reading a book? (Who's)
Which floor is it on?

The imperative

We use the imperative for simple commands, to tell people to do things. The imperative form is the same as the infinitive of the verb.
to touch – Touch the desk.
to stand – Stand up.

Unit Four
Office routine

 Anne and Joy are in their office. They are talking about Joy's daily routine.

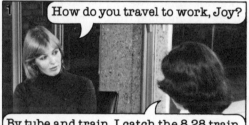

1. **How do you travel to work, Joy?**
By tube and train. I catch the 8.28 train every day and I start work at 9.30.

2. **And how do you spend the day?**
Well, in the morning I take shorthand and type letters.

3. **What time's the coffee break?**
Oh, I make coffee at about 11 o'clock.

4. **And what about lunch?**
I have an hour for lunch. I usually leave between 1.15 and 1.30.

5. In the afternoon I usually make telephone calls, send telexes and do the photocopying.

6. **And what time do you go home?**
5.30 on the dot.

Exercise 44

1 How does Joy travel to work?
2 What time does Joy make coffee?
3 What time does Joy usually go for lunch?
4 How long does Joy have for lunch?
5 What time does Joy usually come back from lunch?

Exercise 45   *Telling the time*

Look at these clocks. In pairs, ask and say what the time is, like this:

A: *Excuse me. Can you tell me the time please?*

B: *Certainly. It's quarter past five.*

Laboratory drill

P: 1. Can you tell me the time please?   R: *It's quarter past five.*

Joy's routine

Exercise 46

Look at these pictures. They show Joy's routine at the office, but they are not in the right order. Listen to Joy describing her routine on the tape. Put the clocks, the notes and the pictures in the right order, like this:

a 9.30 – B start work – picture 2

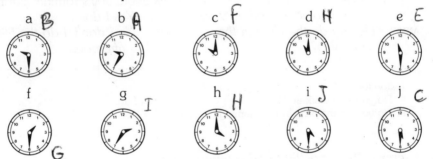

Notes: A open the post; B start work; C go home; D make tea; E type letters; F take shorthand; G have lunch; H make coffee; I send telexes; J do the filing

Laboratory drill

P: Picture 2. What does Joy do at 9.30?   R: *She starts work.*

27

Unit 4

Exercise 47

Answer these questions about Joy's routine with full sentences and write a short passage about what she does at work every day. Use the words in italics in your sentences:

NB   The passage is in the present simple tense (see page 33).

1   What time does Joy start work?

2   What does she do *first*?

3   *Then* what does she do?

4   What time does she make coffee?

5   What else does she do in the morning? (*also*)

6   What time does she have lunch?

7   How does she spend the afternoon? (two things)

8   What time does she make tea?

9   What time does she go home?

Exercise 48

In pairs, pretend you are Anne and Joy. Talk about Joy's routine, like this:

ANNE: *Do you come to work at 9.30?*   JOY: *Yes I do.*
ANNE: *Do you do the filing in the*   JOY: *No I don't. I do the filing in the*
          morning?   *afternoon.*

Laboratory drill
P: Do you start work at 9.30?   R: *Yes I do.*
P: Do you do the filing in the morning?   R: *No I don't.*

Exercise 49   *Spelling and pronunciation*

Write these verbs in the present simple tense third person singular, like this:
take – *takes*

1 take	2 do	3 catch	4 travel	5 work
6 telex	7 go	8 paint	9 drive	10 open
11 type	12 wash	13 photocopy	14 start	
15 send	16 say	17 rise	18 leave	

Now listen to the pronunciation of the final -s on the tape and put the verbs in three columns, like this:

/s/	/z/	/ɪz/
takes	does	catches

Laboratory drill
P: Take   R: *He takes*

28

Exercise 50   *Timetables*

Timetables usually use the 24-hour clock (see page 33). In pairs, pretend you are at a station or a bus stop. Ask about the next train or bus, like this:

A: *Excuse me. What time does the next train leave please?*

B: *Six thirty-nine.*

A: *That's twenty-one minutes to seven. Thank you.*

B: *You're welcome.*

Use these times: 1 0639   2 0849   3 1306   4 2359   5 1615
                 6 0108   7 0425   8 2157   9 1542   10 1934

Laboratory drill A
P: Number 1. What time does the next train leave please?   R: *Six thirty-nine*

Laboratory drill B
P: Train   R: *Excuse me. What time does the next train*
                                              leave please?

Laboratory drill C
P: The train leaves at six thirty-nine.   R: *That's twenty-one minutes to seven.*

Exercise 51   *Journeys*

This map shows the time it takes to travel between Charing Cross, Waterloo and London Bridge by bus, train and tube.

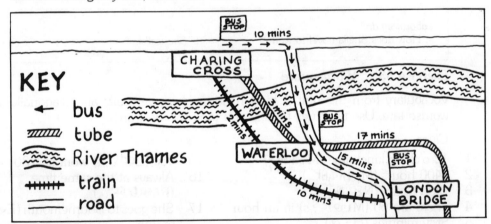

In pairs, talk about the travelling times, like this:

A: *How long does the journey from Waterloo to London Bridge take by train?*

B: *It takes 10 minutes.*

Laboratory drill
P: Waterloo – London Bridge – train
R: *How long does the journey from Waterloo to London Bridge take by train?*

Exercise 52   *Travelling to work*

Look at the pictures of how the BOS staff travel to work every day.

1 Sheila	2 Simon	3 Anne	4 Joy

5 Luisa	6 Fred

In pairs, discuss how they travel to work, like this:

A: *How does . . . travel to work?*   B:

	drives	
He	cycles	
	walks	
		bus
She	goes by	train
		tube

Laboratory drill
P: How does Sheila travel to work?   R: *She walks.*

Exercise 53   *Wordsquare*

Vocabulary from this unit is hidden horizontally, vertically and diagonally in the wordsquare. Use the clues to help you look for the words.

Clues

1 12 o'clock lunchtime (M*idday*)
2 2400 hours (M*idnight*.)
3 1200 hours (N*oon*)
4 There are 60 (M*inute*s) in an hour
5 Sixty minutes (H*our*.)
6 Fred (D*rives*) to work
7 Sheila (W*alks*) to work
8 You (W*ork*) in an office
9 An underground train (T*ub*.)
10 A means of transport (B*us*)
11 Fred drives in his (C*ar*)
12 Joy travels (F*rom*) London
    to Harlow by train
13 I'm going (T*o*) London
14 How do you (T*ravel*) to work?

15 Joy (L*eaves*) work at 5.30
16 Always at the same time
    (R*egularly*.)
17 She goes to Bournemouth (E*very*.)
    month
18 Twenty-four hours (D*ay*.)
19 Not ever (N*ever*.)
20 Opposite of go (C*ome*)
21 I travel (B*y*) train
22 It's Mary's. It's (H*..*.) book
23 An office is a (R*oom*.)
24 You can have this (O*r*) that
25 Joy does the (F*iling*.) after lunch
26 The book is (O*n*) the desk

F	R	O	M	O	M	C	O	M	E
R	I	X	D	R	I	V	E	S	V
E	B	L	M	I	D	D	A	Y	E
G	Y	T	I	L	N	O	O	N	R
U	T	U	N	N	I	C	D	A	Y
L	R	B	U	S	G	W	A	O	N
A	A	E	T	A	H	O	U	R	E
R	V	H	E	R	T	R	T	O	V
L	E	N	W	A	L	K	S	O	E
Y	L	E	A	V	E	S	T	M	R

Exercise 54   *A survey*   Sondage

Look at this chart. It is the result of a survey of how 20 people at BOS travel to work:

	always	occasionally	never	total
bus	IIII	LHT III	LHT III	20
train	III	IIII	LHT LHT III	20
tube	II	IIII	LHT LHT IIII	20
cycle	I	LHT	LHT LHT IIII	20
walk	I	LHT II	LHT LHT II	20
drive	I	LHT I	LHT LHT III	20

In pairs, ask and answer questions about the survey, like this:

A: *How many people always travel by bus?*   B: *Four*
A: *How many people occasionally walk to work?*   B: *Seven*

Laboratory drill A
P: How many people always travel by bus?   R: *Four*

Laboratory drill B
P: Always – bus   R: *How many people always travel by bus?*
P: Occasionally – walk   R: *How many people occasionally walk?*

31

Exercise 55   *A block chart*

Draw a block chart like this and complete it with information from the survey.

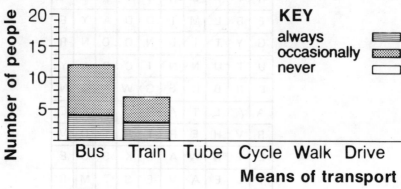

Exercise 56   *A report*

Write a short report on how the BOS staff travel to work. Take your information from the survey, like this:

There are twenty people in the survey. Four people always travel to work by bus, eight people occasionally travel by bus and eight people never travel by bus. . . . etc

NB   One *person* always cycles to work.

A personal letter

> 5 Essex Road
> London SW12 5JL
> 24th October
>
> Dear Janet,
>   Thank you for your letter. I'm always very happy to hear from you. Everything you do is so exciting.
>   I'm sitting here in the office with nothing to do. I'm waiting for 5.30 so that I can go home. Work is very boring at the moment. I do the same things every day. I always get up at the same time in the morning and I travel to work every day by tube and train. I do the same things at work and I usually have lunch in the same canteen. Twice a week I go to the cinema and once a month I go to Bournemouth to see you. Never mind. I'm leaving work next week and I'm getting married in November! At least that's exciting.
>   I look forward to hearing from you soon.
>   Much love,
>   Joy

Exercise 57

Answer these questions about the letter. Use short answers.

1 Who is the letter to? – *Janet.*
2 Who is the letter from?   *Joy*
3 Where does Joy live? *in London*
4 Where does Janet live? *in Bournemouth*
5 What is Joy doing at the moment?
6 What does Joy do at the same time every morning? *s*

7 How does Joy travel to work? *by tube and train*
8 Where does Joy usually have lunch? *in the same canteen*
9 Where does Joy go twice a week?
10 How often does Joy see Janet?
11 When is Joy leaving work?
12 When is Joy getting married? *in november*

Exercise 58

Look at the letter again and look at the business letter on page 14. What are the differences between a personal letter and a business letter?

Language notes

Present simple tense
We use the present simple tense for things we do regularly, always, sometimes, every day, etc.

I/you/we/they	work	type	NB spelling:	go	do	have
he/she/it	works	types		goes	does	has

The question, short answer and negative are made with the present tense of the verb 'to do'.

Question	Short answer	Negative
Do you work?	Yes I do. No I don't.	I don't work.
Does he work?	Yes he does. No he doesn't.	He doesn't work.

Question words
How do you travel to work?
How long does the journey take?
How many people travel by bus?
How often does Joy see Janet?
What time do you have lunch?
When does Joy arrive?

Telling the time

1200 hours – noon, midday
2400 hours – midnight
approximately 12 noon to 5 pm – afternoon
approximately 5 pm to 8 pm   – evening
approximately 8 pm to 6 am   – night
approximately 6 am to 12 noon – morning

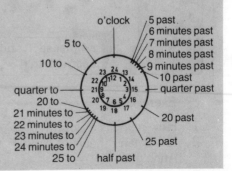

Unit Five
Ordering stationery

 Simon is talking to Anne in their office.

Exercise 59

1 How many is a dozen?
2 How many sheets of flimsy has Anne got?
3 What stationery does Anne need?
4 When is Joy's leaving party?

Exercise 60   *Plurals*

Write the plurals of these words, like this: pen – *pens*

1	box	2	shelf	3	customer	4	sheet of paper	5	secretary
6	filing cabinet	7	glass	8	paper clip	9	telex	10	lunch
11	cup of tea	12	letter	13	floor	14	knife	15	office
16	day	17	man	18	person	19	company	20	woman

NB   There is a note on plurals on page 42

Laboratory drill
P: Pen   R: *Pens*
P: Box   R: *Boxes*

Exercise 61   *Unit nouns*

We usually think of some things in fixed amounts. Decide which word in the list goes with which picture and write about them, like this: *It is a roll of sellotape.*

roll
bottle
box
sheet
glass
jar
packet
cup

NB   Notice the plural of these words:
some bottles of ink

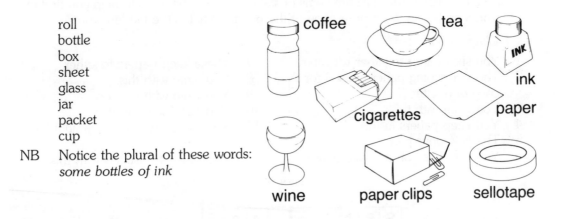

coffee   tea   ink   paper   cigarettes   wine   paper clips   sellotape

Exercise 62   *Count and mass nouns*

Put these words into two lists, like this:
Count   Mass
catalogue   stationery

1	stationery	2	catalogue	3	table	4	desk		
5	bottle	6	tea	7	paper	8	furniture		
9	coffee	10	equipment	11	money	12	filing cabinet	13	car
14	butter	15	envelope	16	paper clip	17	sheet	18	country

Add 2 more words to each list.

NB   There is a note on count and mass nouns on page 41.

Unit 5

Exercise 63 *Planning a party*

Joy and Simon are planning Joy's leaving party. They are making a list of things they need for the party and then discussing what they need to buy. In pairs, discuss the list, as Simon and Joy do:

SIMON: *Have we got any glasses?*
JOY: *Yes. We've got a lot of glasses.*
SIMON: *Have we got any bread?*
JOY: *No. We need some bread.*

PARTY LIST
✓glasses   butter - to buy
bread - to buy   ✓ knives
cheese - to buy   ✓ orange juice
✓plates   wine - to buy

Laboratory drill A
P: Glasses   R: *Have we got any glasses?*

Laboratory drill B
P: Have we got any glasses?   R: *Yes. We've got a lot of glasses.*
P: Have we got any bread?   R: *No. We need some bread.*

Exercise 64 *Hidden word quiz*

All the words in this quiz are items of stationery. Use the clues to help you find the words and write them on a copy of the puzzle. What is the hidden word?

Clues

1 You stick paper together with this.
2 This thin typing paper is used for the copy of a letter.
3 You write with this.
4 You keep papers in this.
5 This is in your pen.
6 You use these on a notice board.
7 These keep papers together.
8 You write with this.
9 You write with this too.
10 You put a letter in this.
11 You measure or draw straight lines with this.
12 You rub out mistakes with this.

HIDDEN WORD

1 SELLOTAPE
2 FLIMSY
3 PENCIL
4 FILE
5 INK
6 DRAWING PINS
7 PAPER CLIPS
8 PEN
9 BALLPOINT
10 ENVELOPE
11 RULER
12 RU

36

Exercise 65   *Numbers*

Listen to the tape. Write down the number referred to in each sentence. Be careful. The number is not always mentioned directly. eg Sentence 1: *12* (midnight)

The stationery cupboard

Charlie Alexander is in charge of the stationery cupboard. He is stocktaking. Here is his list of things in the stationery cupboard:

pencils	H	160	
paper clips	large	120	boxes
ballpoints	blue	148	
sellotape	1"	114	rolls
typing paper	A4	115	reams
files	quarto	150	
rulers	12"	95	

NB   pencils   H = hard   B = soft;   sellotape   1" = wide $\frac{1}{2}$" = narrow;
rulers   12" = long   6" = short
Here is the list of things he needs:

pencils (B)
paper clips (small)
ballpoints (black)
sellotape ($\frac{1}{2}$")
typing paper (quarto)
files (A4)
rulers (6")

Exercise 66

Look at the things Charlie might say to himself:
A: *I need some hard pencils and some large paper clips.*
B: *I do not need any soft pencils or any small paper clips.*
C: *I need some hard pencils, but I do not need any soft pencils.*

Write 2 more sentences like sentence A, 2 more sentences like sentence B and 6 more sentences like sentence C.

Unit 5

☛ **Exercise 67**

Here is the list of stationery Helen needs:

```
6 pencils (B)
2 boxes paper clips (small)
8 ballpoints (black) or blue
2 rolls sellotape (½")
1 ream typing paper (quarto)
5 files (A4)
2 rulers (6")
```

In pairs, ask and reply as Helen and Charlie do:

HELEN: *I need some pencils please.*
CHARLIE: *Right. Hard or soft?*
HELEN: *Soft please.*
CHARLIE: *I'm sorry. I haven't got any.*

Laboratory drill A
P: I need some pencils please.   R: *Right. Hard or soft?*
                                                   or *Right. Soft or hard?*

Laboratory drill B
P: I need some pencils please.   R: *I'm sorry. I haven't got any pencils.*

— **Exercise 68**

Here is Mary's list:

```
6 pencils (H)
3 boxes paper clips (lge)
10 ballpoints (blue)
2 rolls sellotape (1")
3 reams typing paper (A4)
20 files (quarto)
1 ruler (12")
```

In pairs, ask and reply as Mary and Charlie do:

MARY: *Have you got any hard pencils?*
CHARLIE: *Yes. How many do you need?*
MARY: *Six please.*
CHARLIE: *Here you are.*

MARY: *Have you got any large paper clips?*
CHARLIE: *Yes. How many boxes do you need?*
MARY: *Three please.*
CHARLIE: *Here you are.*

Laboratory drill A
P: Have you got any pencils?
P: Have you got any paper clips?

R: *Yes. How many do you need?*
R: *Yes. How many boxes do you need?*

Laboratory drill B
P: Pencils
P: Paper clips

R: *Have you got any pencils please?*
R: *Have you got any paper clips please?*

 Exercise 69

Here is Simon's order for stationery for the sales department:

Internal Order

Brighter Office Supplies Limited

Department:	Sales
Order no:	003926
Date:	27 November 1981
Approved by:	*Sheila Baker*

Quantity	Description	Supplied
3 boxes	paper clips (large)	
1 box	paper clips (small)	
5 rolls	sellotape (1")	
12	pencils (H)	
2	rulers (12")	
6	ballpoints (blue)	
14	files (A4)	
4 reams	typing paper (quarto)	

These are the answers to some questions about the order form. Write the questions, like this:

17 February 1981 — *What is the date on the order form?*
3 — *How many boxes of large paper clips does Simon need?*
A4 — *Does Simon need quarto files or A4 files?*

1	003926	7	2	
2	1	8	long	
3	wide	9	half a dozen	
4	5	10	blue	
5	a dozen	11	14	
6	hard	12	4	

Exercise 70   *Roleplay*

In pairs, pretend to be Charlie and Simon. Simon looks at his order (on this page) and Charlie looks at his stocktaking list (on page 37). Have a discussion about the stationery Simon needs.

Unit 5

Exercise 71 *Conversation*

Write the conversation between Simon and Charlie about the stationery for the sales department. Begin your conversation like this:

SIMON: *Hello, Charlie. How are you today?*
CHARLIE: *Fine thank you, Simon. Can I help you?*
SIMON: *Yes, . . .*

Exercise 72 *An order*

 Listen to the conversation on the tape. Charlie Alexander is talking to Janet Elvin at the warehouse. He is ordering some stationery. Fill in a copy of this order form with the information on the tape.

Order

Brighter Office Supplies Limited

13 Mill Street
Harlow
Essex CM20 2JR

Telephone Harlow 26721
Telex 81259
Cables/Telegrams
BOS Harlow

Order no:

Date: 27 November 1981

To: BOS warehouse
Mallary Street
Croydon

Please supply and deliver:

Qty	Description	Unit price

Deliveries accepted only against our official order
Please quote order no. & date

Signed: .C .Alexander . . . .

Purchasing officer

Standard business letters

Exercise 73

Some business letters are very simple. Look at this standard business letter Simon wrote for Sheila from Sheila's notes:

Notes: tel. conv. this pm / our catalogue / / thanks for yr enquiry / do business with you

The body of Simon's letter:
Further to our telephone conversation this afternoon, I enclose our catalogue.
We thank you for your enquiry and we look forward to doing business with you.

Write the body of these letters in the same way from these notes:

1   tel. conv. this am / our price list / / thanks for yr enquiry / do business with you
2   conv. yesterday pm / a job application form / / thanks for yr enquiry / hear from you
3   tel. conv. this am / a cheque for £97 / / apologise for the delay / receive yr receipt
4   conv. this pm / our invoice / / . . . / receive yr payment
5   yr telex / our official order / / apologise for the delay / receive the goods
6   conv. at yr office / a copy of the financial report / / . . . / hear yr opinion

Exercise 74

Write out in full the short letter Charlie Alexander sent with his official order to the warehouse (see Exercise 72). He addresses the letter for the attention of (Attn:) Mrs Janet Elvin. Use the correct business letter format (see page 14).

Language notes

Count and mass nouns
(also called countable and uncountable nouns)

Count nouns
They have a singular and a plural:

a pencil – { pencils
five pencils
some pencils
the pencil –   the pencils

Mass nouns
They have only a singular *or* a plural (not both):
furniture   scissors
the furniture   the scissors
some furniture   some scissors

Negative

With count nouns: There are not *any* pencils.

With mass nouns: There is not *any* furniture.

Question

With count nouns: Are there *any* pencils?

How many pencils are there?

With mass nouns: Is there *any* furniture?

(Are there any pieces of furniture?)

How much furniture is there?

(*How many* pieces of furniture are there?)

Plurals (of count nouns)

typewriter + s = typewriters

table + s = tables

ending -o, -ss, -ch, -sh, -x *ending -f, -fe*

box + es = boxes shelf + ves = shelves

lunch + es = lunches knife + ves = knives

glass + es = glasses

ending consonant + y

secretary + ies = secretaries

BUT day + s = days (vowel + y)

NB paper clip – paper clips

filing cabinet – filing cabinets

cup of tea – cups of tea

Irregular (add to this list of irregular plurals when you meet them)

man – men

woman – women

person – people

Adjectives

Adjectives do not change in English: He's a *good* boy.

He's *good*.

They are *good* boys.

Have got

I have got two pencils. (I've got . . .)

He has got two pencils. (He's got . . .)

Question: Has he got any pencils?

How many pencils have you got?

Negative: He has not got any pencils. (He hasn't got . . .)

NB *Have got* is not used in speech. The formal written form is *to have* eg I have two pencils. Does he have any pencils? He does not have any pencils.

Consolidation Unit A
Your news and news extracts

Your News – *the radio programme for you*
and News Extracts – *interesting articles from the newspapers*

Exercise 75 *Headlines*

 Listen to the news headlines on the tape. Put these headlines in the order in which you hear them:

1 SALESMAN OF THE YEAR
2 THE COST OF LIVING
3 THE VALUE OF THE POUND
4 UNEMPLOYMENT
5 THE WEATHER
6 PEACE TALKS
7 BRITISH SUMMER TIME ENDS
8 SUPERSONIC JET TIMETABLE

Exercise 76 *Radio news*

 Write short answers to these questions about the news headlines:

1 Which two countries are taking part in the peace talks?
2 At what rate are wages rising, 7% or 10%?
3 When is the jet's first scheduled flight to New York?
4 How much is $2.26 worth in pounds sterling?
5 How many people are out of work?
6 What does Mr Smith do?
7 What time do the clocks go back?
8 In which country is it raining?

Exercise 77 *Salesman of the year*

 Can you find eight differences between the newspaper article *Salesman of the year* on page 45 and the radio article on the same subject?

Exercise 78 *Car number spot*

 Listen to the car number spot on the tape. Write down the six car numbers. What is the telephone number to ring for a prize?

Exercise 79 *Summer time*

Look at the article on British summer time on page 45. Write ten questions about the time throughout the world, like this:
When it is two o'clock in Alexandria, what time is it in Rome?
What time is it in Sydney when it is quarter past six in Hong Kong?

Give your questions to somebody else in the class. Write short answers to the ten questions you are given.

Consolidation Unit A

Exercise 80   *The weather*

Pretend it is yesterday. Look at the weather table and write ten sentences about the weather round the world, like this:
It is warm and cloudy in Amsterdam today.

NB   Cold = below 15°C/60°F; warm = 15–25°C/60–75°F; hot = over 25°C/75°F

Exercise 81   *Exchange rates*

Write ten questions about the conversion table, like this:
What are 43.75 Yugoslavian dinars worth in Norwegian kroner?

Give your questions to someone else in the class. Write short answers to the questions you are given.

Exercise 82   *Britain*

Answer these questions about the article *Focus on Britain*.
1   What is another name for Great Britain?   It is the United kingdom
2   Which four countries does the United Kingdom consist of?
3   What is the population of Britain?
4   What is the area of Britain?
5   What is another name for the European Economic Community?
6   Who are Britain's main trading partners?
7   What are Britain's main visible exports?
8   What are Britain's main invisible exports?

Exercise 83   *Abbreviations*

Can you find the abbreviations for these words in the news articles on page 45?
1   avenue   4   degree   7   mister   9   pound
2   Centigrade   5   Fahrenheit   8   October   10   television
3   company   6   limited
And do you know what these abbreviations stand for? The answers are all in the news articles on page 45.
11    $ 12   approx.   13   %   14   m   15   sq   16   k
17   GB   18   UK   19   pm   20   EEC

Exercise 84   *Focus on Italy*

Look at the article *Focus on Britain*. Use this information to write a similar article about Italy:
– consists of the mainland, Sardinia, Sicily, Elba and many other islands
– has frontiers with France, Switzerland, Austria and Yugoslavia
– EEC member
– capital city: Rome
– total area: approx. 324,000 sq k
– population: the same as GB
– main trading partners: West Germany, France, N. America
– main exports: machinery, cars, iron and steel

Exercise 85   *A timetable*

Write five sentences about the Concourse timetable using these verbs:
to depart (from), to leave, to take off (from), to arrive (at), to land (at).
Write the times out in full eg *twenty-five to one* (not 1235).

Salesman of the Year

Mr John Smith of Inskip is this year's winner of the 'Salesman of the Year' award. Fifty-three-year-old John works for Smiths Marketing Co. Ltd. and he travels to work every day by train. Mr and Mrs Smith and their daughter, Rachel, are going to London to collect their prizes – a colour TV and a bottle of champagne.

British summer time ends

For those of you who regularly telephone other countries, we bring you a handy guide to the international time zones. When it's noon in London, this is the time in the rest of the world.

Alexandria 2pm

Delhi 10.30pm

Hong Kong 8pm

Los Angeles 4am

Nairobi 3pm

New York 7am

Rio de Janeiro 9am

Rome 1pm

Tokyo 9pm

Sydney 10pm

Concourse timetable

British Airflight today announce the new daily timetable for the supersonic jet plane Concourse between four major cities.

London	d 1000	New York	a 1335	New York	d 1515	London	a 2045
London	d 1505	Delhi	a 2210	Delhi	d 1620	London	a 2325
Delhi	d 2330	Sydney	a 0640	Sydney	d 0750	Delhi	a 1455

FOCUS▷ ON BRITAIN

Starting today we bring you the facts about different countries. Of course, you know about Great Britain, don't you? Check!

The United Kingdom (also called Great Britain) consists of four countries – England, Scotland, Wales and Northern Ireland. It has a population of approximately 56 million people and an area of about 240,640 square kilometres. London is the capital city. Britain is a member of the European Economic Community (also called the Common Market) and its main trading partners are the EEC countries and North America. Britain's main exports are cars, machinery, textiles and chemicals and its invisible exports include banking, insurance and tourism. Britain's North Sea oil also makes it one of the world's oil producers.

Yesterday's weather around the world . . .

		°C	°F
Amsterdam	C	16	61
Athens	S	30	86
Berlin	F	19	66
Cairo	F	24	75
Copenhagen	C	10	49
Lisbon	S	28	82
London	Fg	17	63
Madrid	S	28	82
Paris	R	22	72
Rome	S	31	88
Stockholm	Sn	3	37
Tokyo	F	14	59

C = cloudy; F = fine;
Fg = foggy; R = raining;
S = sunny; Sn = snowing

CONVERSION TABLE

What is your £ worth?

Austria .... 30 schillings
France .... 9.51 francs
Germany .... 4.11 marks
Greece .... 79.75 drachma
Italy .... 1,810 lire
Japan .... 490 yen
Norway .... 11.30 kroner
Spain .... 148.50 pesetas
United States .... 2.26 dollars
Yugoslavia .... 43.75 dinars

'Water

Personnel Competition

Read these five sentences about the people in the picture:

1 The four people in the front row are the sales representative, the personnel manager, the sales manager and the managing director (not in that order!)

2 The managing director's personal secretary is behind her boss.

3 The secretary is next to the managing director's personal secretary and behind the personnel manager.

4 The receptionist is on the right and the secretary is on the left in the back row.

5 The sales manager is in front of the sales assistant.

Questions:

1 Who is in front of the receptionist?
2 Who is next to the receptionist?
3 Which two people is the managing director between?

Send your answers with your name and address on a postcard to:

Gay Haines, PERSONNEL COMPETITION, PO Box 52, Trafalgar Square, London SW1 3XY
Closing date for entries: 30 Oct 1981

Unit Six
Joy's leaving party

 The BOS staff are all at Joy's leaving party.

Exercise 86

1 Who is the girl with glasses?
2 Where is Howard?

3 Who smokes and who does not?
4 What are they giving Joy?

Unit 6

Joy's leaving party

Exercise 87

Using the words from these tables, write six true sentences about the people in the picture at Joy's leaving party, like this:
A woman with short fair hair is talking to a man with a pipe and a moustache.

A The	woman	is	talking sitting standing	to next to near	a the	man
	man					woman

with	short	dark	curly	hair	and	a pipe a moustache
						a beard *barbe*
	long	fair	straight			glasses

Exercise 88

In pairs: One person thinks of one of the people in the picture. The other person must guess who it is by asking questions, but the first person can only answer *yes* or *no*.
eg. A: *Is it a man?*   B: *Yes.*
  A: *Is he drinking?*   B: *No.*
  A: *Has he got a moustache?*   B: *No.*
  A: *Is he standing next to a lady with dark hair?*   B: *Yes.*

NB *Is it a man with a moustache? (Several men have got moustaches.)*
  Is it the man with a moustache? (Only one man has got a moustache.)
  If your partner makes a mistake and asks, 'Is it the man with a moustache?', you can answer, 'Which one? There are two/three men with moustaches.'

Laboratory drill
P: Is it the man with the moustache?
R: *Which one? There are two men with moustaches.*

Exercise 89   *Which man?*

 Listen to the tape. A female customer wants to talk to one of these men at BOS. Which one?

1   Tony   2   Brian   3   David   4   Michael   5   John   6   Richard

At the buffet table

This is the buffet table at Joy's leaving party. The cheese sandwiches are next to the cake and the crisps are between the peanuts and the wine. The orange juice is in front of the wine and the pieces of cheese are in front of the sandwiches.

Exercise 90

Simon is offering things to Anne. In pairs, offer and reply like this:

1   SIMON: *Would you like* {*a cheese sandwich?*
some crisps?
a cigarette?}

ANNE: {*Yes please. I'd love* {*one.*
some.}
No thank you. Not at the moment.}

2   SIMON: *Would you like something to* {*eat?*
drink?}

ANNE: *Yes please.*
SIMON: *What would you like?*
ANNE: *A* {*piece of cake*
glass of wine} *please.*

NB   You can say *a piece of cake/a piece of cheese*
or *some cake/some cheese,*
a glass of wine/a glass of orange juice
or *some wine/some orange juice*

Laboratory drill A
P: Would you like a cheese sandwich?   R: *Yes please. I'd love one.*
P: Would you like some crisps?   R: *Yes please. I'd love some.*

Laboratory drill B
P: A cheese sandwich   R: *Would you like a cheese sandwich?*

Unit 6

Exercise 91 *Hidden word puzzle*

Use these clues to help you fill in a copy of this puzzle and find the hidden word. The answers are all days of the week.

Clues

1 The day before Thursday.
2 The day after Monday.
3 The day before Tuesday.

4 The day between Wednesday and Friday.
5 The day before Sunday.
6 The day before Saturday.

HIDDEN WORD

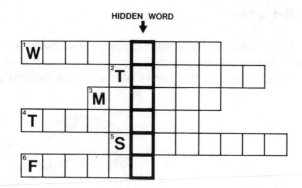

Going out

Exercise 92

This is Simon's diary. He would like to go out with Anne. There are suggestions for places to go in his diary. In pairs, invite Anne out as Simon does and reply as Anne does:

SIMON: *Would you like to go to the theatre with me on Monday?*
ANNE: { *Yes. I'd love to.*
         { *I'm sorry. I'm busy on Monday.*

MON to	go to the theatre?	THU	have lunch?
TUE to	have dinner?	FRI	go to a disco?
		SAT	come to Jane's party?
WED to	see a film?	SUN	drive to the seaside?

Laboratory drill
P: Monday. Go to the theatre

R: *Would you like to go to the theatre with me on Monday?*

Exercise 93

Mary and Helen are discussing what they would like to do together this week. Take your ideas from Simon's diary. Make suggestions and reply as Mary and Helen do:

MARY: *Let's go to the theatre together on Monday.*
HELEN: { *That's a good idea.*
{ *I'm sorry. I'm busy on Monday.*

NB You must say: 'Let's *go* to Jane's party . . .'

Laboratory drill
P: Monday. Go to the theatre

R: *Let's go to the theatre together on Monday*

nom interrogatif

Allons à ------

In a restaurant

Exercise 94

Simon and Anne are in a restaurant. Listen to their conversation on the tape and write down what they both had to eat. This is the menu:

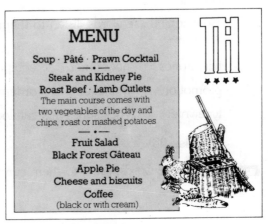

MENU

Soup · Pâté · Prawn Cocktail
— • —
Steak and Kidney Pie
Roast Beef · Lamb Cutlets
The main course comes with two vegetables of the day and chips, roast or mashed potatoes
— • —
Fruit Salad
Black Forest Gâteau
Apple Pie
Cheese and biscuits
Coffee
(black or with cream)

Exercise 95

In pairs, order a meal from the menu like this:

WAITER: *What would you like to start with?*
CUSTOMER: *Soup please. And then I'd like steak and kidney pie with chips.*
WAITER: *And for dessert?*
CUSTOMER: *I'd like fruit salad please.*

Laboratory drill A
Answer the waiter and order the first item in each section on the menu.

Laboratory drill B
Answer the waiter and order the second item in each section on the menu.

Laboratory drill C
Answer the waiter and order the third item in each section on the menu.

Unit 6

Pronunciation – Word stress

Exercise 96

Look at these words and listen to the tape:

O o
jumper

o O
supplies

Now copy these words, listen to them on the tape and mark the stress in the same way:

glasses	machine	filing	Wednesday	upstairs
office	canteen	moustache	question	answer

NB Most two-syllable words have the same stress as jumper. Think of five more.

Exercise 97

Look at these three-syllable words and listen to the tape:

O o o
cinema

o O o
description

Now copy these words, listen to them on the tape and mark the stress in the same way:

telephones	newcomer	equipment	September	envelopes
promotion	manager	ordering	department	furniture
typewriter	enclosure	catalogue	Saturday	assistant

Exercise 98

Copy these words, listen to them carefully and mark their stress pattern, like this:

O o
filing

director	representative	cabinet	invitation
coffee	receptionist	personal	application
orange	advertisement	personnel	nationality

Exercise 99

Copy these phrases, listen to them carefully and mark their stress pattern, like this:

O o   o o o
filing cabinet

There is only one main stress in each phrase.

orange juice	managing director	coffee pot
personal secretary	personnel officer	per cent
sales representative	sales assistant	in-tray

Listen to Exercises 96 to 99 again and say the words with the same stress.

52

Personal invitations

Look at this invitation and the reply:

```
John and Susan invite you to a party
at 33 Honister Avenue, Newcastle NE2 3PA
on Saturday 7th November
at 8 pm
RSVP
```

> 7 Park Avenue
> Newcastle NE1 4AJ
>
> 2nd November
>
> Dear John and Susan,
> Thank you very much for your invitation
> to the party on 7th November. I'd love
> to come.
> I look forward to seeing you both.
>   Love, Carolyn.

NB   To refuse an invitation you can write:
Thank you very much for your invitation to the party on 7th November.
I'm afraid I have a previous engagement for that evening.
I look forward to seeing you at another time.

Exercise 100

Reply to this invitation:

> 109 Claxton Grove
> Newcastle NE1 5JD
> 2nd November
>
> Dear John and Susan,
>
> Would you like to come to dinner on
> Wednesday 11th November at 7.30 ?
>
> We look forward to seeing you.
>
> Love, David & Ann

Exercise 101

Write an invitation to a party or dinner and send it to someone else in the class.
Reply to the invitation you receive.

Unit 6

Language notes

Articles
Is it *a* man? (Any man)
Is it *the* man with a moustache. (A particular man)

He's a very tall man. He's the tall *one* over there.
Would you like a sandwich? Yes please. I'd love *one*.
Would you like some sandwiches? Yes please. I'd love *some*.

Would like

You He They	would like 'd like	something. to do something.

Question: Would you like {something? / to do something?}
What would you like?
What would you like to do?
Negative: I wouldn't like to go out.

54

Unit Seven
The ideal secretary

 Mary Mackie is on a television programme. The presenter is Michael Walton.

1 Good evening, ladies and gentlemen. Welcome once again to 'World at Work'.

2 Tonight in the studio we've got the winner of this year's 'Ideal Secretary' competition, Mary Mackie. Hello, Mary.

Hello, Michael.

3 Mary, what makes an ideal secretary?

Well ... er ... she can type and take shorthand and

4 That's right, Mary. Is there anything else?

Yes, she's well-dressed and efficient and never late for work. And of course ...

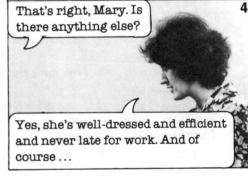

5 That's wonderful, Mary. Well, there you are, viewers, the ideal secretary.

Can I just say ...

6 Thank you Mary. Congratulations and goodnight.

Goodnight, but ...

Exercise 102

1 What is the television programme called?
2 Why is Mary on the programme?
3 Is Mary always on time for work?
4 What are the people who watch television called?
5 Is Michael Walton a pleasant man?

55

Exercise 103   *A survey*

Imagine that your class is the sales department of BOS Ltd. Tomorrow some important French buyers are coming to the company. You need urgently to translate your advertising material into French. Pretend you are Simon Young and ask 12 people in the class about things they can do to help, like this:

A: *Can you* {*speak French?*
       type?
       use the photocopier?

B: {*Yes I can.*
      No I can't.
      Not very well.

Other people will ask you what you can do. Fill in the results of your survey on a copy of a questionnaire, like this:

Name	speak French	type	use the photocopier
Simon	No	Yes	Yes
Anne	not very well	Yes	Yes

Laboratory drill A
P: Speak French   R: *Can you speak French?*

Laboratory drill B
P: Speak French   R: *I can speak French.*

Laboratory drill C
P: Speak French   R: *I can't speak French.*

Exercise 104   *A memo*

Write a memo to Sheila Baker from Simon Young telling her the results of the survey. Use the correct memo format and begin your memo like this:
Here are the results of the survey:
Four people can speak French well, five people cannot speak French very well and three people cannot speak French at all.

The Ideal Secretary – and her lucky boss

Mary Mackie, who lives in Epping, is the winner of this year's 'Ideal Secretary' competition. Her prizes are a typewriter, a cassette recorder and a weekend in Paris.

Miss Mackie works in Harlow for Brighter Office Supplies Ltd. She is twenty-nine and single. Her boss is BOS managing director, Fred McLean.

Mr McLean says, 'Mary is the ideal secretary. She's friendly and very efficient. Her shorthand speed is 140 wpm and her typing speed is 70 wpm. She can speak two foreign languages, French and German. She is never late for work . . . .and she makes very good coffee.'

Mary says, 'It's easy to be a good secretary when you've got a good boss.'

NB   wpm = words per minute

Exercise 105   *A news article*

Here are some answers to questions about the article. Write the questions using these question words: *Who? Where? What? How . . .?*
eg Mary Mackie – *Who is the winner of this year's Ideal Secretary competition?*

1 Epping
2 A typewriter, a cassette recorder
   and a weekend in Paris
3 In Harlow

4 Twenty-nine
5 Fred McLean
6 Two – French and German

Laboratory drill A
P: Mary's a secretary.

R: *Is Mary a secretary?*

Laboratory drill B
P: Mary makes good coffee.

R: *Does Mary make good coffee?*

Laboratory drill C
P: Mary is on the television programme.
  Why

R: *Why is Mary on the television programme?*

P: Mary comes from Epping. Where

R: *Where does Mary come from?*

Exercise 106   *Qualities*

In small groups, decide which of these qualities are appropriate to a 'perfect boss' and which are appropriate to an 'ideal secretary'. Some qualities might be appropriate to both.

He/she is: pleasant ambitious intelligent efficient reliable
               considerate hard-working polite well-dressed attractive
               helpful

He/she can: plan type organise take shorthand make decisions
              prepare reports speak foreign languages give speeches

Use sentences like this:

A:	*It*	*is* *is not*	*important that a*	*boss* *secretary*	*is . . .* *can . . .*

B: *I agree. / Yes it is. / No it's not. / I don't agree.*

Can you think of any other qualities which make someone a good boss or a good secretary?

Exercise 107   *Radio programme*

Jacques de la Plaine is the winner of this year's 'Perfect Boss' competition. Make a short radio or television programme about him. The programme presenter can interview Jacques and his secretary. There is some information about Jacques on page 6. You can make up other information about him.

Exercise 108   *News article*

Write a short newspaper article about Jacques de la Plaine – the 'Perfect Boss'.

Exercise 109   *To give*

Look at the word order with the verb *to give*. All these sentences are correct:

They are giving Mary a prize.   *They are giving a prize to Mary.*
They are giving her a prize.   *They are giving a prize to her.*
They are giving it to Mary.   *They are giving it to her.*

Write the words in these sentences in the right order:

1 him give please book the
2 always gives presents her he
3 to me please it give
4 Joy they giving present to a are
5 present Joy they giving are a
6 typewriter Christmas for him a giving is she
7 him to she gives sometimes them
8 you give can me file the please

Laboratory drill
P: They're giving Mary a prize. Her   R: *They're giving her a prize.*
P: A typewriter.   R: *They're giving her a typewriter.*

Exercise 110   *Differences*

Anne works in the office with Simon now and it is slightly different. Look back at the picture of the office on page 13 for *one minute*. Then look at this picture of the office.

In pairs, talk about the things that are different, like this:
There weren't 4 books on the bottom shelf.
The pot plant was on the filing cabinet. Now it's on the table.
There was a photocopier on the table. Now there isn't.

NB   *Was* is the past tense of *is.*
     Were is the past tense of *are.*

> *Laboratory drill*
>
> P: A photocopier on the table
>
> R: *There was a photocopier on the table. Now there isn't.*
>
> P: Six books on the top shelf
>
> R: *There were six books on the top shelf. Now there aren't.*

Exercise 111   *Experience*

Listen to the tape about three people who are looking for jobs. Make notes about them by filling in a copy of this chart. Be ready to write down the spelling of their names.

Standard

name	experience	typing	switchboard	shorthand	other notes
David Richards	X N	N	X	N	
caroline Bennett	⊗ N	X	X	X	at sec. college
Lorraine welder	X	X	X	N	

Exercise 112   *Job advertisements*

Look at these job advertisements in a newspaper. Decide which person in Exercise 111 is suitable for which job. It does not matter if you do not understand every word in the advertisements.

Evening Star CLASSIFIED
64 Fleet Street, London EC4J 6BB

Positions Vacant

RECEPTIONIST
Can you use a PMBX switchboard?
Are you polite?
Have you got a good telephone manner?

A well-known firm of accountants needs an experienced receptionist. Typing preferred but not essential. Good pay and good working conditions. Write to: Helen Ferns, Box 6390.

SECRETARY Efficient secretary wanted to work in a small friendly office. Experience is not essential if you can type and take shorthand. Reasonable starting salary. Good promotion prospects. Ring 854 5246 or write to: Neil Warner, Preston Goods, 37 Highgate Road, Preston, Lancs PR2 4LN.

FILING CLERK/PERSON FRIDAY Large industrial firm requires a filing clerk/person Friday to help in a large office. If you're intelligent, qualifications are not important. Send details to: Daniel Milgrom, Box 2061.

Letters of recommendation

Exercise 113

 David Richards is applying for the job of filing clerk/person Friday advertised in the Evening Star. The principle of his school, Oliver Howard (Bay House School, 19 Ingleborough Road, Birkenhead, Cheshire L42 6RD) is writing a letter of recommendation for him. He is dictating the letter to his secretary. Listen to the tape and write the letter. Use the correct business letter format. These are the words in the letter (without any punctuation or capital letters):

dear mr milgrom thank you for your letter of 2nd november i am very happy to give david richards a reference for the job of filing clerk person friday he is cheerful pleasant and helpful in class and he is intelligent and also efficient in his work i can certainly recommend him for the job yours sincerely

Exercise 114

Write a letter of recommendation for Carolyn Bennett from Brian Keith of Laws Secretarial College (13 Canonbury Lane, Inskip, Lancs PR4 2EL). Carolyn is applying for the job of secretary advertised in the Evening Star.

Language notes

Modals: can

I He	can do it.

Negative: He cannot do it. (He can't . . .)

Question: Can you do it?
What can you do?
You can do it, can't you?

Short answer: Yes I can. No he can't.

Personal pronouns

I you he she it we they	can see is/are giving it to	me you him her it us them

---

Unit Eight
Appointments

 Helen is Howard Spencer's secretary in the personnel department. She is talking on the phone in her office.

Exercise 115

1 What time is Paul Sawyers meeting Mr Spencer?
2 What is Mr Spencer already doing on Thursday?
3 Which afternoon is Mr Spencer taking off?
4 Why is he having lunch with his wife on Thursday?

Exercise 116　*Appointments*

Today is Monday. This is a page from Sheila Baker's diary for this week. In pairs, ask and answer questions about what Sheila is doing this week, like this:

SHEILA:

What am I doing
Am I doing anything

{ today?
tomorrow?
on Wednesday?
at the weekend?

ANNE:　*You're seeing Mr Smith at 10 o'clock this morning and Mr Parker at 11. You're not doing anything at lunchtime. You're going to a board meeting this afternoon at 2 o'clock.*

NB　We use the present progressive tense to talk about definite appointments or arrangements in the future.

Laboratory drill

P: Am I doing anything this morning?　R: *You're seeing Mr Smith at 10 o'clock and Mr Parker at 11.*

P: And what about lunch?　R: *You're not doing anything at lunchtime.*

Exercise 117　*Arranging an appointment*

Marisa Balzarini wants to make an appointment to see Sheila Baker this week. Fill in Anne's half of this telephone conversation. Take your information from Sheila's diary.

MARISA:　*Hello. Can I make an appointment to see Sheila Baker, please? She knows I'm coming this week.*

ANNE:　.~~yes~~.. ~~~~ which day ?

MARISA:　*Thursday, if possible. Is she free in the morning?*

ANNE:　I'm afraid . ~~you~~ ~~are~~ attending ,, sales conference in Brighton
　　　　　　　　　　　　　　　　she is

MARISA:　*Well, how about Tuesday?*

ANNE:　I'm sorry. She . is. seeing mister Matthew an she is visiting the new
　　　　　　　　　　　　　　　　　　　　　　　　　　　warehouse

MARISA: *No. I can't meet her for lunch today or on Wednesday.*
ANNE: *..wednesday she is free for lunch*
MARISA: *Well I'm free in the morning, but I'm entertaining some customers in the afternoon.*
ANNE: *..it isn't possible this week*
MARISA: *Oh well then, I suppose it must be next week.*

> *Laboratory drill*
> Say Anne's part of the dialogue on the tape. There is more than one correct answer. Just say what you think Anne says.

Things to remember

Exercise 118

Helen often forgets to do things.
This is her list of things to do today:

> *Remember!*
> send a telex to New York
> phone Mr Parker
> write to Mr Jones
> order the stationery
> type a letter to Miss Negus
> photocopy the report
> do the filing
> make an appointment to see Chris Foord
> give the order to Simon

In pairs, talk about the things she must do, like this:

A: { *What must she do?*
    { *What's she got to do?*

B: *She's got to* ⎫
   She must   ⎬ *send a telex to New York.*
   She has to   ⎭

> *Laboratory drill A*
> P: Send a telex to New York   R: *She's got to send a telex to New York.*
>
> *Laboratory drill B*
> P: Send a telex to Paris   R: *She must send a telex to Paris.*
>
> *Laboratory drill C*
> P: Send a telex to Cairo   R: *She has to send a telex to Cairo.*

Exercise 119

Write your own list of things to do in the next few days. Discuss your lists in pairs.

Exercise 120 *Dates*

Say and write these dates as they are in Britain and as they are in the United States, like this:

1/5/42 – UK *(the) first (of) May nineteen forty-two.*
– US *(the) fifth (of) January nineteen forty-two.*

1	5/9/84	3	12/12/79	5	7/4/81
2	2/8/65	4	3/6/82	6	15/10/90

NB   There is a note on dates on page 67.

Laboratory drill A
P: The first of May.   R: *May the first.*

Laboratory drill B
P: January the fifth nineteen forty-two.   R: *The fifth of January nineteen forty-two.*

Laboratory drill C
P: September   R: *In September*
P: September the fifth   R: *On September the fifth.*

Exercise 121 *A calendar*

Look at the BOS calendar. In pairs, talk about the important dates like this:
A: *When's the sales conference?*   B: *It's on (the) 12th (of) November.*
A: *When's the stocktaking?*   B: *It's from (the) 17th to (the) 19th (of) November.*

─── CALENDAR ───

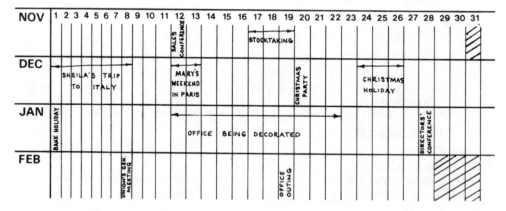

Laboratory drill
P: When's the sales conference?   R: *It's on the twelfth of November.*
P: When's the stocktaking?   R: *It's from the seventeenth to the nineteenth of November.*

Exercise 122   *A map of Harlow*

Listen to the conversation between Anne and Simon on the tape. Use these words to fill in a copy of the key:

BOS   Post office   Supermarket   Newsagent's   Bank   Cinema

NB   Which side of the road do people drive on in England?

Exercise 123   *Asking the way*

You are at the station. In pairs, ask your way to places on the map and say how to get there, like this:

A: *Excuse me. Can you tell me the way to the newsagent's please?*
B: *Certainly. Go straight ahead. At the roundabout take the second exit. Then take the first road on the left. The newsagent's is on the left.*

You can ask questions starting from other places on the map too.

> *Laboratory drill*
> P: The newsagent's   R: *Excuse me. Can you tell me the way to the newsagent's please?*

Exercise 124   *Where am I?*

This time start from the station again. Tell your partner how to get to a place on the map, but DO NOT TELL HIM/HER WHERE HE/SHE IS GOING. Then your partner must say where he/she is, like this:

A: *Go straight ahead. At the roundabout take the second exit. Then take the first road on the left. It's on the left. Where are you?*
B: *At the newsagent's.*

> *Laboratory drill*
> P: You are at the station. Go straight ahead. At the roundabout, take the second exit. Then take the first road on the right. Which building is on the left?
> R: *BOS. Figure E*

Exercise 125   *Expressions of time*

It is midday on Saturday 7 November 1981.
Decide which phrase on the left refers to which time on the right, eg 1–c

1	this morning	a	1982
2	the day before yesterday	b	December 1980
3	last weekend	c	10 am Saturday 7 November 1981
4	next month	d	11 pm Friday 6 November 1981
5	last December	e	Saturday 7 November 1981
6	today	f	10 pm Saturday 7 November 1981
7	tomorrow afternoon	g	Monday 9 November 1981
8	the day after tomorrow	h	Thursday 5 November 1981
9	yesterday evening	i	3 pm Sunday 8 November 1981
10	tonight	j	December 1981
11	next year	k	6 pm Friday 6 November 1981
12	last night	l	Saturday 1st and Sunday 2nd November 1981

Letter writing

Exercise 126

This letter was torn up and thrown away by mistake. Put the pieces in the correct
order and rewrite the letter using the correct format.

NB   Five small pieces of the letter are missing. Fill in the missing words.

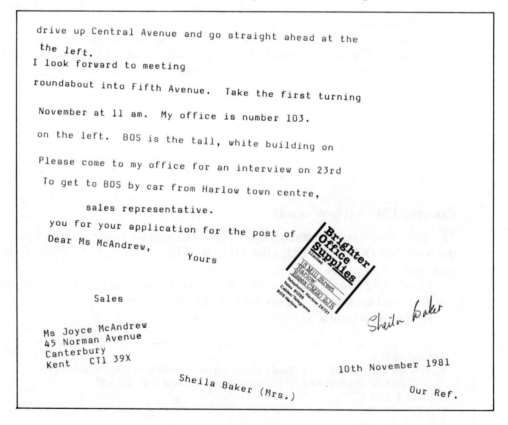

```
   drive up Central Avenue and go straight ahead at the

    the left.
 I look forward to meeting

roundabout into Fifth Avenue.  Take the first turning

November at 11 am.  My office is number 103.

on the left.  BOS is the tall, white building on

Please come to my office for an interview on 23rd

 To get to BOS by car from Harlow town centre,

     sales representative.
  you for your application for the post of
  Dear Ms McAndrew,
                      Yours

       Sales

   Ms Joyce McAndrew
   45 Norman Avenue
   Canterbury
   Kent   CT1 39X
```

Brighter Office Supplies Limited
13 Mill Street
Harlow
Essex CM60 24R
Telephone Harlow 81200
Cables Harlow 28721
BOS Harlow

Sheila Baker

Sheila Baker (Mrs.)

10th November 1981

Our Ref.

Exercise 127

Give short answers to these questions about the letter.
1 Who is the letter to?
2 Who is the letter from?
3 Who do you think typed the letter?
4 Where does Joyce McAndrew live?
5 Is Joyce McAndrew married?
6 Is Sheila Baker married?
7 When is Joyce McAndrew's interview?
8 What job does Joyce McAndrew want?
9 Is Joyce McAndrew travelling by train or car?
10 What colour is the BOS building?

Exercise 128

Sheila Baker wrote a similar letter to another applicant for the job, Rachel Snell (93 Lee Road, London SE3 4XB). Her appointment is after Joyce McAndrew's at 11.45. Write the letter and explain how to get to BOS from the station.

Language notes

Obligation

She must do it.
She has to do it.
She has got to do it. (She's got . . .)
Question: What must she do?
What has she got to do? (What's . . .)

Dates

The months are: *January (Jan), February (Feb), March (Mar), April (Apr), May, June, July, August (Aug), September (Sep), October (Oct), November (Nov), December (Dec).*
There is a difference between the written and spoken form of dates:

Written	Spoken
3rd Jan/3rd January 3 Jan/3 January	the third of January/January the third
NB 3/1/52	(UK) the third of January nineteen fifty-two (US) the first of March nineteen fifty-two

Notice the prepositions we use with dates and times:

In 1981   *On* (the) 23rd   *At* the weekend
In December   *On* Friday   *At* 5 o'clock
In the morning   *At* lunchtime
NB   Yesterday evening. Last Friday. Next weekend. (no preposition)

Unit Nine
Job satisfaction

 Mary, Simon, Anne and Helen are having lunch together in the BOS canteen.

1 Well, Anne. This is the end of your first month at BOS. How do you like it?

2 I love it. I really enjoy secretarial work.

Secretarial work is boring. I don't like typing or filing or taking shorthand . . .

3 . . . but I need the money.

What's the matter, Mary?

4 I'm not feeling very well. I've got a terrible headache. I think I've got a cold.

5 You should go to bed. Why don't you take the rest of the day off.

6 That's a good idea.

Some people have all the luck!

Exercise 129

1 How long ago did Anne join BOS?
2 What does Helen think about secretarial work?
3 What is the matter with Mary?
4 Helen thinks someone is lucky. Who?

Exercise 130 *Problems and suggestions*

These three people in BOS have got problems. In pairs, have short conversations
giving them suggestions, like this:

SIMON: *What's the matter, Helen?*
HELEN: *I haven't got any money.*
SIMON: {*Why don't you borrow some?*
          {*You should borrow some.*
HELEN: *That's a good idea.*

I haven't got any money.

Suggestions
borrow some
see your bank manager
work in the evenings

Suggestions:
go home
lie down
take an aspirin

I've got a terrible
headache. I think I've
got a cold.

Can you think of any other suggestions?
Think of suggestions for Simon's problem:

I've got to get an
urgent message to
someone in Germany.

Laboratory drill A
P: Borrow some   R: *Why don't you borrow some?*

Laboratory drill B
P: Go home   R: *You should go home.*

Likes and dislikes

Exercise 131

Helen does not like being a secretary. These are all things she says to Simon
about her job. Write sentences like this:

1   I write a lot of letters but I *don't like it.* – *I don't like writing letters.*

2   I answer the telephone all day long and I'm *fed up with it.*
3   I take shorthand *every day* and I *can't stand it.*
4   I use the photocopier a lot and I *don't like it.*
5   I type all day long and I *hate it.*
6   I open the mail *every morning* and I'm *bored with it.*
7   I write memos all the time and I'm *tired of it.*
8   I go home on Fridays and I *love it.*

Laboratory drill
P: I write a lot of letters and I don't like it.   R: *I don't like writing letters.*

Exercise 132

Mary, Anne, Simon, Helen and Sheila are having lunch together. They are sitting round a circular table and talking about what they like and what they do not like about their jobs. Each person likes one thing and does not like one thing. Use the information in the sentences to fill in a copy of this diagram and then answer the questions.

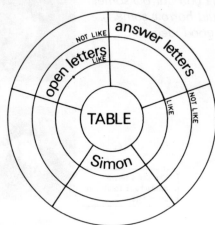

Information

1 Sheila is sitting between Anne and Mary.
2 The person on Simon's right does not like using the telephone and the person on Simon's left likes going home.
3 Sheila likes meeting people and Simon does not like filing.
4 Anne is sitting on Helen's left.
5 The person on Sheila's right does not like typing and the person on Sheila's left likes writing letters.
6 Helen is sitting on Simon's left. Mary is on Simon's right.

Questions

1 Who likes working at BOS?
2 Who does not like taking shorthand?

Exercise 133

In pairs, ask and answer questions about the diagram, like this:
A: *Who doesn't like taking shorthand?*
B: *Jenny.*
A: *What does Simon like?*
B: *Going to the cinema.*

NB These are not the correct answers!

Laboratory drill A
P: Open letters   R: *Who likes opening letters?*

Laboratory drill B
P: Take shorthand   R: *Who doesn't like taking shorthand?*

Exercise 134

Look at this table. It shows the results of a small survey about how Anne, Mary and Helen feel about their jobs.

	LOVE	LIKE	NOT LIKE	HATE
FILE		A	M	H
TYPE	A	M	H	
TAKE SHORTHAND		A	M	H
BE SECRETARY	A M		H	
WORK FOR BOS	A M	H		

Confirm your opinion about the results like this:

A: *Anne likes filing, doesn't she?*
A: *Helen doesn't like typing, does she?*
A: *Helen hates taking shorthand, doesn't she?*
A: *Mary loves being a secretary, doesn't she?*

B: *Yes she does.*
B: *No she doesn't.*
B: *Yes she does.*
B: *Yes she does.*

Laboratory drill A
P: Anne likes filing, doesn't she?
P: Helen doesn't like typing, does she?

R: *Yes she does.*
R: *No she doesn't.*

Laboratory drill B
P: Anne likes filing.
P: Helen doesn't like typing.

R: *Anne likes filing, doesn't she?*
R: *Helen doesn't like typing, does she?*

Exercise 135

Play this game with a friend. Ask him/her the questions, like this:
A: *Do you like meeting people?*   B: *Yes I do.*
A: *Do you like music?*   B: *No I don't.*

Follow the arrows and when you reach a number, look at the jobs on the next page. Give your friend advice about a job, like this: *You should be a musician.*
If the answer to any question is 'I don't know', advise your friend to try doing the last thing you asked about, like this: *Try working with animals.*

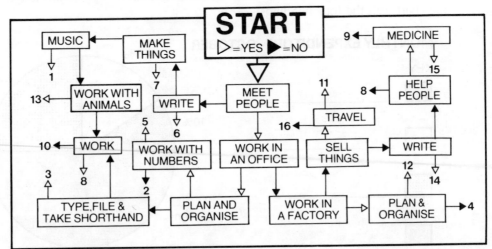

Unit 9

Look here for your job from Exercise 135
1   musician   2   manager in an office   3   secretary
4   manual worker in a factory   5   accountant   6   writer
7   craftsman   8   Can you think of a job you'd like?   9   social worker
10   not work   11   salesman   12   factory manager
13   farmer or vet   14   journalist or writer   15   doctor or nurse
16   shopkeeper or shop assistant

Laboratory drill
P: Meet people   R: *Do you like meeting people?*

Exercise 136   *Petty cash*

Simon adds up the petty cash each week. All the money comes under four
headings: *postage, travel, stationery, sundries.*
Listen to the tape and fill in the amount spent under each heading in October on
a copy of this table.

OCTOBER	postage	travel	stationery	sundries	
First week					
Second week					
Third week					TOTAL
Fourth week					EXPENDITURE
TOTAL					

Fill in the totals. What was the total amount of petty cash spent in October?

NB   There are 100 pence in £1 (one pound).

Exercise 137   *Pie chart*

Sheila wants to know what the petty cash is spent on, so Simon draws her a pie
chart. Look at the figures in the table above and fill in a copy of this key to the
pie chart with the four headings.

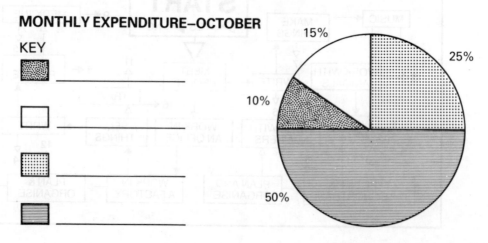

MONTHLY EXPENDITURE—OCTOBER

KEY

Time and motion study

Exercise 138

Do a time and motion study on how Anne spends her working day. Start by reading this description:

> She starts work at 9.30 and leaves at 5.30. She has an hour for lunch. She types for about one and a half hours every morning and for about an hour in the afternoon. She does the filing for about half an hour a day and spends the same amount of time taking shorthand. Making tea or coffee takes about a quarter of an hour and she does it twice a day. She spends about an hour and a half on the phone. The rest of the time she spends doing other things, such as talking to people, opening the mail, reading the newspaper etc.

1   How long does Anne spend at work each day (including her lunch hour)?
2   How long does she spend doing each of these things per day?
typing – filing – shorthand – phone – tea/coffee – lunch – miscellaneous (everything else)
3   What percentage of her time does she spend doing each thing?

NB   This formula will help you calculate percentages:

$$100 \times \frac{\text{amount of time in one activity}}{\text{total amount of time}}$$

eg $100 \times \dfrac{1 \text{ hour}}{8 \text{ hours}} = \dfrac{100}{8} = 12\frac{1}{2}\%$

Draw a pie chart with a key showing the percentage of time she spends on each activity. Remember that a circle has $360°$.

Exercise 139

Look at your pie chart. Ask and answer questions about the percentage of time Anne spends on each activity, like this:
A: *How much time does she spend typing?*
B: *She types for 31% of the time.*
A: *How much time does she spend at lunch?*
B: *She's at lunch for . . .*

NB   Notice how we say fractions on page 76.

Laboratory drill
P: How much time does Anne spend typing?
R: *She types for thirty-one and a half per cent of the time.*

Brighter Office Supplies
Limited

REPORT ON EXPENDITURE AT HEAD OFFICE 16th November 1981

Findings

Comparative figures for the following items last year and this
year are:

	1980	1981
rent & rates	£34,100	£34,100
light & heat	£60,000	£63,000
telephone	£44,000	£48,900
telexes & cables	£ 9,000	£ 9,500
postage	£53,200	£54,000
stationery	£42,900	£44,700
photocopying	£ 4,900	£ 5,800
petty cash	£ 2,900	£ 4,300

Conclusions

The rent and rates are not going up. We can control the figures
which are going up. Petty cash costs are going up because people
are using petty cash to buy stamps and stationery.

Recommendations

We should save money and we should ask the staff to save money.
Possible savings are:
- to use the telephone after 1 pm when it is cheaper
- not to make personal telephone calls at work
- to switch off lights when people go out of the office
- to use carbon paper, not the photocopier
- to order stationery from the warehouse, not to buy it on petty cash
- to send post to the post room, not to buy stamps on petty cash
- to re-use envelopes

Peter Hall, Accounts department

Exercise 140   *Hidden word puzzle*

Use these clues to help you fill in a copy of this word puzzle and find the hidden
word. All the words are in Peter Hall's report.

Clues

1 Suggestions
2 Written description of a situation
3 The 'facts' in a report
4 Money kept in an office for small
  payments
5 Not business (eg phone calls)
6 Money you pay out

7 Ways of spending less money
8 Numbers
9 You use this coloured paper to make
  copies
10 Money paid regularly to the owner of
  a building for its use
11 Local government tax on buildings

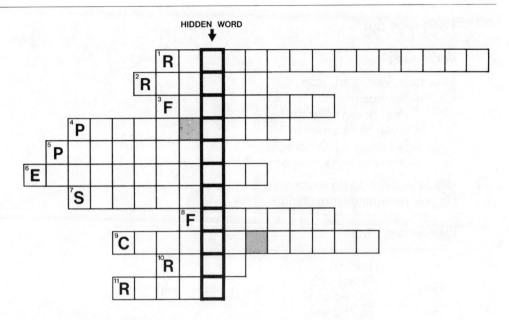

Exercise 141   *A memo*

Write a memo to the staff from Peter Hall about his findings on expenditure.
Suggest ways they can save money, like this:
Please do not leave the lights on.
Please use the phone after 1pm.

Laboratory drill
P: They should use the phone after one pm.   R: *Please use the phone after one pm.*
P: They shouldn't leave the lights on.   R: *Please don't leave the lights on.*

Exercise 142   *A survey and a report*

Do a survey to find out what time people would like to start work (or school).
Ask questions like this:
What time do you start work?
Do you like starting work at 9 o'clock?
What time would you like to start work?

Ask similar questions about leaving work.

Present your findings as a graph or chart. Write a short report making
recommendations. Lay out your report properly.

Unit 9

Language notes

Verbs + ing

Like, hate, love, start, stop
e.g.   I like typing.
       Simon doesn't like typing.
       Do you like typing?
       What do you like doing?
       Anne likes filing, doesn't she?

NB   *Would* you like *to do* (something)?
     Do you like *doing* (something)?

Expressions + ing

He's	tired of bored with fed up with	doing (something).
He	can't stand	

Suggestions

Why don't you do (something)?
You should do (something).
Please do (something)/Please do not do (something).

Fractions

$12\frac{1}{2}$ twelve and a half
$33\frac{1}{3}$ thirty-three and a third
$66\frac{2}{3}$ sixty-six and two thirds
$31\frac{1}{4}$ thirty-one and a quarter
$18\frac{3}{4}$ eighteen and three quarters
$\frac{1}{5}$ a fifth
$\frac{4}{5}$ four fifths

Unit Ten
Job applications

 Howard Spencer is interviewing an applicant for the job of salesman.

1 Now Mr Oswald ... you went to America in 1962.

1963 actually.

2 And what did you do in America?

Well, I was a salesman, but I didn't sell office equipment.

3 What did you sell?

Telephone equipment. I worked for the telephone company.

4 Oh yes. That's on your C V too. That's quite satisfactory. Now, would you like to know anything else about the job?

5 No. I read the job description carefully before I came. I'd like to work for BOS.

6 Good. Because you've got the job. When can you start?

Exercise 143

1 When did Mr Oswald go to America?
2 How long did he work in America?
3 Did he sell stationery?

4 Who did he work for?
5 Did Mr Oswald get the job with BOS?

Unit 10

The past simple

Exercise 144

Write these verbs in the past simple tense:

1	look – *looked*	5	work	9	wash	13	file
2	move	6	order	10	photocopy	14	open
3	wait	7	stop	11	end	15	start
4	visit	8	walk	12	type	16	stay

 Listen to the verbs on the tape and put them into three columns according to the sound of the ending.

/t/	/d/	/ɪd/
look*ed*	mov*ed*	wait*ed*

> *Laboratory drill*
> P: Look   R: *Looked*

Exercise 145

Make sentences about things which happened some time ago, like this:

1 It is Friday. I (want) the stationery last Friday. *I wanted the stationery a week ago.*
2 It is 1981. Peter (work) for BOS in 1979.
3 It is May. He (stop) work in January.
4 It is 10.05. I (answer) the telex at 10.00.
5 It is Monday. They (travel) to Scotland last Monday.
6 It is 11 o'clock. Simon (open) the mail at 10 o'clock.
7 It is November. Mr Passas (visit) BOS in October.
8 It is Thursday. Simon (post) the letter on Tuesday.

> *Laboratory drill A*
> P: I wanted the stationery last Friday. When   R: *When did you want the stationery?*
>
> *Laboratory drill B*
> P: I want the stationery. A week   R: *I wanted the stationery a week ago.*

Exercise 146   *Late for work*

Tell the story in the past tense using the notes. The notes are not in the right order.

a   He (wake up) at 11 o'clock.
b   Then he (hear) the church bell.
c   One morning Fred McLean's alarm clock (not go off).
d   It (be) Sunday.
e   He (see) a taxi, but there (be) someone in it.
f   He (knock) on the door, but no-one (be) there.
g   He (go) to the bus stop and (wait) for a bus, but the bus (not come).
h   He (put on) his clothes and (run) out of the house.
i   So he (run) to work.

Cover the notes and tell the story again just looking at the pictures.

Laboratory drill
P: Picture 1   R: *One morning Fred McLean's alarm clock didn't go off.*

Exercise 147   *Anne's day*

Anne now does the same things as Joy did when she worked for BOS. Look
back at Joy's routine on page 27. Last Wednesday Anne followed the same
routine. In pairs, talk about what Anne did, like this:
A: *What time did she start work?*   B: *9.30.*
A: *What did she do first?*   B: *She opened the post.*

Laboratory drill A
P: Picture 2. Did Anne start work at 9.30?   R: *Yes she did.*
P: Picture 6. Did she do the filing first?   R: *No she didn't.*

Laboratory drill B
P: Picture 2. What did Anne do at 9.30?   R: *She started work.*

Exercise 148   *Who*

Notice the difference between these two questions with *Who*:
John saw Mary.   A: *Who saw Mary?*   B: *John.*
                        A: *Who did John see?* B: *Mary.*

Make questions from these sentences, like this: The answer is in brackets.
Sheila phoned Fred at 10 o'clock. (Fred). *Who did Sheila phone at 10 o'clock?*

1   Sheila phoned Fred at 10 o'clock. (Sheila)
2   Simon went to the bank on Wednesday. (Simon)
3   Simon asked Joy. (Joy)
4   Joy asked Simon. (Joy)
5   The accountant wrote the report. (The accountant)
6   They liked Helen. (Helen)

Laboratory drill A
P: *John saw Mary.*   R: *Who saw Mary?*
P: *John saw Mary.*   R: *Who did John see?*

Laboratory drill B
P: *Who saw Mary?*   R: *John saw Mary.*
P: *Who did John see?*   R: *John saw Mary.*

Unit 10

Exercise 149　*A curriculum vitae*

 Listen to the tape and fill in a copy of this CV for Lorraine Welder. Some details are already written in for you.

CURRICULUM VITAE
(Please write in block capitals)

Surname: ....
First name(s): ....
D.o.b.: ....
Marital status: ....
Children: ....

Address: ....
.....13 QUEEN'S CRESCENT
.....LONDON SW1T 5JJ
Tel no: ....

Education and further studies

Dates	Schools/colleges (name and address)	Qualifications
		GCE O LEVELS
	PRESTON PARK 6ᵀᴴ FORM COLLEGE, PRESTON, LANCS.	
		SECRETARIAL DIPLOMA

Experience

Dates	Place of work (with address)	job	pay

Names and addresses of three referees:

MS E SPINK, LONGFORD SECRETARIAL COLLEGE, BRIGHTON, SUSSEX BR9 4RD

MR J CHAMBERS, CHAMBERS TRUCKS, 33 JEVINGTON ROAD, BRIGHTON, SUSSEX BR2 50B

MR S MAYER, BUFFALO BOOKS, 29 BAKER STREET, LONDON N1F 4AB

NB　In England many schoolchildren do GCE (General Certificate of Education) examinations. The exams are at two levels – Ordinary (O level) and Advanced (A level).

Exercise 150   An interview

Here is Lorraine Welder's interview with Helen Ferns for the job of receptionist advertised on page 59. Write down what you think Lorraine said. Use her curriculum vitae for information.

HF: *Now then, Mrs Welder . . . I see you went to school in York from 1964 to 1968.*

LW: . . . . . .

HF: *Oh yes. Sorry. And how many O levels did you get?*

LW: . . . . . .

HF: *And did you get any A levels?*

LW: . . . . . .

HF: *That's right. You got a secretarial diploma, didn't you? What did you do when you left secretarial college?*

LW: . . . . . .

HF: *Then you moved to London, didn't you? What did you do there?*

LW: . . . . . .

HF: *When did you leave?*

LW: . . . . . .

HF: *Oh really? Did you have a boy or a girl?*

LW: . . . . . .

HF: *That's nice. He must be quite big now. Er . . . How much did you earn at Buffalo Books?*

LW: . . . . . .

HF: *I see. Have you got any references?*

LW: . . . . . .

HF: *That's all very satisfactory, Mrs Welder. Now is there anything you'd like to know about the job?*

> *Laboratory drill*
> Say Lorraine's part in the dialogue. There is not one correct answer. Just say what you think Lorraine says.

Exercise 151   Questions

Lorraine asked six questions about her new job. What were they?

What		my office?
How long	are	my boss?
When	do	the salary?
Where	can	I start work?
Who	is	I start the job?
What time		the holidays?

Exercise 152   Roleplay

Write your own curriculum vitae. You can make up the details or write your real CV. In pairs, ask and answer questions about your CV as if at a job interview. Apply for one of the jobs on page 59 or take a job advertisement from a newspaper.

Unit 10

Letters of application

Exercise 153

This is the letter of application Lorraine Welder wrote for the job of receptionist (the advertisement is on page 59). Decide which verb in this list goes in which space in the letter:

apply – can – enclose – gave – go – growing – had – hearing – left – like – look – see – saw – use – worked – would

---

13 Queen's Crescent
London SW1T 5JJ

27 November 1981

Ms Helen Ferns
Box 6390
Evening Star
64 Fleet Street
London EC4J 6BB

Dear Ms Ferns,

I ...¹saw.. your advertisement in the Evening Star and I would ..²like.. to ..go³... for the job of receptionist.
I ..⁴enclose.. a full curriculum vitae. As you can ..⁵.... I
..⁶.... as a receptionist before I ..⁷.... children. I
can ..⁸.... a PMBX switchboard and I ..⁹.... type.
Buffalo Books ..¹⁰.... me a very good reference when I
..¹¹.... my job. Now my two children are ..¹².... up and
I ..¹³.... like to ..¹⁴.... back to work.

I ..¹⁵.... forward to ..¹⁶.... from you.

Yours sincerely,

L. Welder.

Lorraine Welder (Mrs)

82

Exercise 154

Write a letter of application for one of the other two jobs advertised on page 59. The letter can be from Carolyn Bennett, David Richards or you.

Exercise 155 *Hidden word puzzle*

Use the clues to help you fill in a copy of this puzzle and find the hidden words. All the words are verbs in this unit in the past tense.

Clues

1 She . . . for a job as a receptionist.
2 I didn't . . . the alarm clock.
3 Did you . . . Simon yesterday?
4 He . . . . his clothes.
5 Did the alarm clock . . . . ?
6 He . . . for a bus for an hour.
7 He . . . work at 5.30.
8 He . . . on the door.
9 He . . . telephone equipment.
10 He didn't . . . . until 11 o'clock.

Hidden word: You use it to tell a story.

Language notes

Past simple tense

We use the past simple tense to tell stories about the past. We also use it when the time *when* something happened is important.

Regular verbs
work + ed = worked
type + d = typed
stop + p + ed = stopped

I/you/he/she/it/we/they   worked   typed

The question, short answer and negative are made with the past tense of the verb 'to do'.

Question
Did you type it?
You saw him, didn't you?
Where did he work?
Who typed it?
Who did you see?

Short answer
Yes I did. No I didn't.

Negative
I didn't type it.

Irregular verbs			
	Past simple	*Question*	*Negative*
to be	I was you were he/she/it was we were they were	Was I . . .? Were you . . .?	I wasn't . . . You weren't . . .
have got must has to $\Big\}$ have got to	I had . . . I had to . . .	Did you have . . .? Did you have to . . .?	I didn't have . . .
can	I could . . .	Could you . . .?	I couldn't . . .

Other irregular verbs in this unit

to come – came
to do – did
to get – got
to go – went
to have – had
to hear – heard
to leave – left
to make – made
to put – put

to read – read
to run – ran
to see – saw
to sell – sold
to send – sent
to take – took
to wake – woke
to write – wrote

See also the list of irregular verbs on page 139.

Consolidation Unit B

Your news and news extracts

Your News – *the radio news programme for you*
and News Extracts – *interesting articles from the newspapers*

Exercise 156   *The USA*

Here are some answers to questions about the article *Focus on the USA* on page
87. Write the questions, like this:

> 13 – *How many states were there originally in America?*
> or *How many horizontal stripes are there on the American flag?*

1 Washington DC
2 50
3 1000 AD
4 Christopher Columbus

5 Virginia
6 1774
7 4th July
8 George Washington

Exercise 157   *Hidden word puzzle*

Use the clues to help you fill in a copy of this word puzzle and find the hidden
word. All the words appear in the article '*Biscuit strike over*'.

Clues

1 The money workers earn is called their . . .
2 Whitaker's make biscuits in their . . .
3 Workers are getting a pay . . . of £5 per week.
4 The workers are not at work. They are on . . .
5 People like to work in good working . . .
6 The company is *giving* the workers *more* money.
7 The bosses of a company are called the . . .

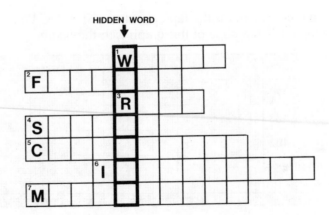

85

Exercise 158   *Raise/rise; found/find*

Do not confuse these verbs:
to *raise* something: (regular; past tense – *raised*) = to put something up
to *rise*: (irregular; past tense – *rose*) = to go up
to *find* something: (irregular; past tense – *found*) = to discover something that is already there
to *found*: (regular; past tense – *founded*) = to start something new

Fill in the correct verb in these spaces:
1 He . . . the company in 1920.
2 People do not . . . many colonies now.
3 He . . . all the prices in his shop.
4 The cost of living . . . every year.
5 . . . your hand.
6 I looked for my pencil, but I didn't . . . it.
7 I . . . my ruler though.
8 Prices . . . last year by 10%.

Financial Times Index

Exercise 159

Look at the graph and write about last week's FT index, like this:
On Monday the index opened at 475. It rose sharply by 1.5 points to 476.5 at lunchtime and then fell slightly. The market closed at 476.

Use these words:

fall go down ↓ drop	sharply	by (5) points	to (475.5)
↑ go up rise	slightly		

Exercise 160

Listen to the news item on the tape about the FT index. Write down the figures from the tape. Fill in a copy of this graph with the figures.

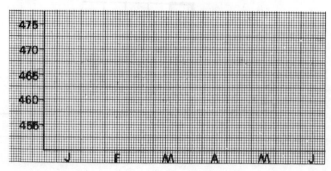

FOCUS ▷ ON THE USA

The second in our series of facts about different countries.

The USA is a Federal Republic which consists of 50 states and the Federal District of Washington DC (its capital). Originally there were only 13 states. The American flag (sometimes called the 'stars and stripes') consists of 13 horizontal stripes and 50 stars.

Leif Ericsson first discovered America in about 1000 AD, but the Italian, Christopher Columbus, rediscovered it in 1492. The Cabot brothers, from England, reached Newfoundland (the *new found land*) in 1497. This is now part of Canada, but the British and other Europeans soon founded colonies further south. For example, Sir Walter Raleigh started the first British Colony, Virginia, in 1585. This became one of the original thirteen states of the USA.

The war of Independence from Britain started in 1774. Congress passed the Declaration of Independence on 4th July 1776 (the Americans still celebrate Independence Day on 4th July every year), but fighting did not stop until 1781. George Washington became the first president of the US in 1789.

Guest Keen	164	+16
Hongkong (Selangor)	912	+137
ICL	51	+8
Jerome S Hldgs	120	+30
Lev F J C	157	+15
Lyle Shipping	373	+25
Mercantile House	660	+38
Newhold & Burton	59	+11
Rothmans	80½	+1
Royal Bank of Scot.	166	+3
Sino Pacific Pet.	60	−9
Thomson T-Line	50	−1
Thorn EMI	374	+2

Biscuit strike over

The strike at Whitaker's biscuit factory ended yesterday when the management agreed to increase wages and improve working conditions. Workers are getting a pay rise of £5 per week.

PRIZE PUZZLE

This week's puzzle is about international trade. Find out:

– Which nationality is each company?
– What does each company produce?
– Where does each company export its products?

Your information

The Japanese company does not produce machinery
The German company trades with Brazil
The company which produces cars trades with Britain
The Italian company produces chemicals

Your question

Which company trades with France?

Send your answer on a postcard by 7th July 1981 to: Prize Puzzle: International Trade, 24 Printing House Square, London EC4 5DG

...but, above all, they sell ... their fuel economy — much of which comes from the advanced aero-

...sals but 1980s and there is a quest mark over McDonnell Douglas.

LAST WEEK'S FT INDEX

Consolidation Unit B

Radio news

Exercise 161

Listen to the news programme on the tape. Are these statements true or false?
1   The interest rates are going up.   True/False
2   The members of OPEC are all industrial countries.   True/False
3   The workers at Jones Bros want more money.   True/False
4   Mr Jones is on strike.   True/False
5   Sir Alan Smith lived in Surrey.   True/False
6   An accident is blocking a road junction.   True/False
7   The Financial Times index rose in February.   True/False
8   There was a bomb scare in a London store.   True/False

Exercise 162

Listen to the news programme again and choose the correct answer to these questions.
1   What is the minimum lending rate now?
    a $1\frac{1}{2}$%   b   12%   c $13\frac{1}{2}$%   d $30\frac{1}{2}$%
2   What is the good news for savers?
    a   High lending rates   b   Low lending rates
    c   High interest rates   d   Low interest rates
3   What are the oil producing countries discussing?
    a   OPEC   b   oil prices   c   the cost of living
    d   industrial countries
4   Are Jones Bros going to raise their workers' wages?
    a   Yes   b   No   c   Probably   d   Probably not
5   How old was Sir Alan Smith when he retired?
    a   14   b   45   c   70   d   84
6   Which street is one-way?
    a   Brazilian Way   b   Italian Grove   c   Denmark Hill
    d   Egyptian Street
7   What was the FT index when the Stock Exchange closed on the last day of June?
    a   455.4   b   10   c   3.2   d   468.6
8   Which one of these sentences is not true?
    a   A bomb went off in a London store.
    b   Mrs Anne Roach works in a London store.
    c   Mrs Roach went shopping in her lunch hour.
    d   Mrs Roach left her sandwich-box under her desk.

Exercise 163   *Bomb scare*

Listen to the news item on the tape about the bomb scare. Write about what happened in your own words. What do you think happened next? Write two or three more sentences to complete the news item.

Exercise 164   *Traffic news*

Listen to the traffic news on the tape.
1 Which letter marks the accident?
2 Which letter marks the road works?
3 Which street is one-way?
4 How do you get from point 1 to point 2 on the map? Complete the instructions you cannot hear clearly on the tape:
Motorists who must drive through the centre of town should turn . . . at the roundabout in Italian Grove and use . . . and . . .

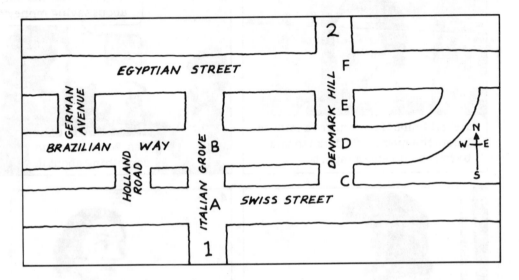

Exercise 165   *Newspaper project*

Make a class newspaper. You can publish articles you have written for homework or you can write new articles. You can publish information about yourselves, your work or your school. You can conduct a survey and publish the results.

These words might give you some more ideas (look up words you do not know in a dictionary or discuss them with your teacher):

advertisements
cartoons and jokes
cinema and theatre announcements
classified ads
crime
crossword
currency exchange rate
diary of forthcoming events
drawings
financial pages
general features
horoscopes
interviews

leader article
letters to the editor
news stories
personal column
photographs
puzzles
recipes
reviews of books, plays, TV, music, etc
sport
stories
TV and radio programmes
weather report
woman's page

Unit Eleven
A meeting

 Fred is talking to Sheila in her office just before they go to a meeting.

1 Hello, Sheila. Have you got a minute before the meeting? I'd like to talk to you about Peter's report.

2 Do you mean the one about saving money?

Yes. We've got to do something about it.

3 Well, some customers haven't paid their bills yet. I'll send them reminders.

4 Good. And I've seen the bank manager about borrowing some more money.

5 I wonder ... could you write a memo to the staff about saving money ... or have you already done it?

6 Well, I haven't written one, but don't worry. Peter has.

Exercise 166

1 What would Fred like to talk about?
2 What was Peter's report about?
3 What has Fred done at the bank?

4 Who has written the memo to the staff?

Polite requests

Exercise 167

Here is a list of things Howard asked Helen to do:

> phone Mr Smith
> send the telex to New York
> write to Paul Sawyers
> photocopy the report
> type the letters
> give the memo to Sheila
> do the filing
> ask Ms Matthews to come in

In pairs, ask and answer as Howard and Helen do:

HOWARD: *Could you phone Mr Smith please?*
Would you phone Mr Smith please?

HELEN: *Certainly, Mr Spencer. I'll phone him at once.*

NB *Could you* . . . and *Would you* . . . are more polite than *Can you* . . .
We use the *will* future for a decision made at that moment about the future
(see page 96).

Laboratory drill A
P: Phone Mr Smith   R: *Could you phone Mr Smith please?*

Laboratory drill B
P: Phone Mr Smith   R: *Would you phone Mr Smith please?*

Laboratory drill C
P: Could you phone Mr Smith please?   R: *Certainly. I'll phone him at once.*

Exercise 168

Fred asked Mary to do the same things. In pairs, ask and answer as Fred and
Mary do:

FRED: Could ⎱   you phone Mr Smith please?
          Would ⎰

MARY: ⎰ *I've already phoned him.*   (some time before now)
          ⎱ *I've just phoned him.*   (a few moments ago)

Laboratory drill A
P: Could you phone Mr Smith please?   R: *I've already phoned him.*

Laboratory drill B
P: Could you phone Mr Smith please?   R: *I've just phoned him.*

Unit 11

Exercise 169

Helen looks back at her list the next day. She has not done any of the things.
Talk about the list again, like this:
HELEN: *I'm afraid I haven't phoned Mr Smith yet.*
HOWARD: *Could you phone him immediately please?*

> *Laboratory drill*
> P: Phone Mr Smith   R: *I'm afraid I haven't phoned Mr Smith yet.*

A meeting

Exercise 170

The managers of BOS Ltd are having a meeting. They are looking at the
company's progress since 1978. Fred is making a speech. These are his notes for
the speech:

> last May / open a branch in Liverpool
> 2 years ago / start a pension scheme for the employees
> sell a record number of desks in 1978
> hire 50 more employees in January
> in 1979 / raise our prices by 7%
> give £3,000 to charity last year
> increase sales by 10% in 1980

Fred thinks the time when all these things happened is important so he is
speaking in the past simple tense. Express interest in the things Fred says,
like this:
A: *Last May we opened a branch in Liverpool.*
B: *Oh. So we've opened a branch in Liverpool.*

You are more interested in *what* has happened and how it affects the company
now rather than *when* it happened, so you use the present perfect tense.

> *Laboratory drill*
> P: Last May we opened a branch in Liverpool.
> R: *Oh, so we've opened a branch in Liverpool.*

Exercise 171

After Fred's speech, the other people at the meeting question him about the
things he said. They remember what has happened, but they cannot remember
when. Ask Fred about the things he said, like this:
A: *You say we've opened a branch in Liverpool. Could you tell us when
    exactly?*
B: *Certainly. It was last May.*

Laboratory drill
P: We opened a branch in Liverpool.
R: *You say we've opened a branch in Liverpool. Could you tell us when exactly?*

Exercise 172   *Word puzzle*

Fill in a copy of the puzzle and find the missing words in these sentences. They are all adverbs of time which we use with the present perfect tense.

Clues
1 I've . . . done the filing.
2 I haven't written any of these letters . . ..
3 I've . . . finished typing the report.
4 I haven't seen him . . . 1978.
5 I've . . . been to Rome.
6 Have you . . . used a photocopier?
7 Of course I've used a photocopier . . ..

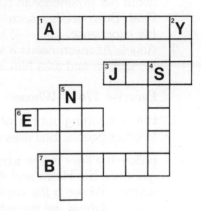

Experience

Exercise 173

When Anne applied for the job at BOS she had an interview with Howard Spencer. This card shows her secretarial experience.
Listen to the tape and mark a tick (√) on a copy of the card for things Anne has done before and a cross (×) for things she has not done before.

take shorthand		work a switchboard	
take the minutes at a meeting		type reports	
use a photocopier		order stationery	
send a telex		keep a petty cash book	

Exercise 174

In pairs, talk about Anne's experience, like this:
HOWARD: *Have you taken shorthand before?*
ANNE: {*Yes I have.*
        {*No I haven't.*

Laboratory drill A
P: Take shorthand   R: *Have you taken shorthand before?*

Laboratory drill B
P: Have you taken shorthand before?   R: *Yes I have.*
P: Have you taken the minutes at a
   meeting before?   R: *No I haven't.*

Unit 11

Exercise 175 *Roleplay*

1 Brian Bean is starting a business selling sand to Egypt. A newspaper reporter is interviewing him about his experience in this sort of business. Think about the experience Brian needs and then have an interview.
Here are some notes to help you:
do any market research? – sell anything before? – go to Egypt? – know anything about Egypt? – why sell sand?
2 Angela Atkinson is starting a business exporting spaghetti to Italy. Interview her about her experience in business and why she is doing it.
3 Brian Bean needs a secretary. He interviews Carolyn Clarke and asks her about her experience.
4 Angela Atkinson needs a salesman to go to Italy. She interviews David Donaldson and asks him about his experience.

Exercise 176 *Whose?*

Helen is sorting out her office and she has found a lot of stationery that belongs to other people. She asks Anne who the things belong to.

Follow the lines to see who the things belong to. In pairs, ask and answer questions like Helen and Anne:

HELEN: *Whose is the stapler?* ANNE: *It's ours.*
Whose are the rubber bands? *They're hers.*

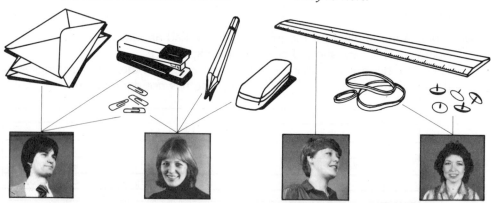

> *Laboratory drill*
> P: *It's my ruler.* R: *It's mine.*

Exercise 177 *Who's/whose?*

These two questions are sometimes confused.
Who's = Who is . . .? or Who has . . .?
Whose = Who does this belong to?

Fill in the correct question word in these sentences:

1 . . . going to Greece?
2 . . . rubber is this?
3 . . . in room 405?
4 . . . met Mr Passas?
5 . . . telephone is broken?
6 . . . been to Rome?

Exercise 178   *Punctuation*

One of the BOS designers has designed a new typewriter model.
Listen to the tape. He is explaining where all the punctuation marks are. Fill in these punctuation marks on the typewriter keyboard (only the keys with punctuation marks are shown).

!	apostrophe	.	full stop (period in US)
*	asterisk	-	hyphen, dash
( )	brackets	" "	inverted commas, quotation marks
:	colon	/	oblique
,	comma	?	question mark
!	exclamation mark	;	semi-colon

NB   Listen carefully to the pronunciation of *apostrophe*.
There is a note on the use of some punctuation marks on page 97.

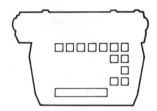

Exercise 179   *Capital letters*

Which of these words are normally written with a capital letter? (See note on page 97).

day – john – atlantic ocean – nineteenth – was – river – i – mr spencer – typewriter – italian – monday – he – pm – bos ltd – milgrom & co – egypt – month – sea – see – mount everest – river thames – ten – paris – it – december – english

Letters of enquiry

Exercise 180

Oliver Howard is dictating a letter to his secretary (you can find his address in Exercise 113). Listen to the tape and write the letter. Use these notes to help you:
see your advertisement for office equipment in Evening Star/please send full catalogue and price list

Exercise 181

Write the body of three more letters of enquiry using these notes:
1   *hear about your typewriters from the Commercial Attaché at the British Embassy/please send more information about them*
2   *talk to your representative about your equipment/please send brochure showing your range of desks*
3   *see your publicity material about your range of stationery/please send your representative to visit us*

Language notes

Present perfect tense

We use the present perfect tense for a past action. What happened and its effect on the present is more important than when it happened.

have + past participle   eg: I have typed it.   (I've . . .)
                              He has seen her.   (He's . . .)

Question	Short answer	Negative
Have you typed it?	Yes I have. No I haven't.	I haven't typed it.
What has he done?		He hasn't seen her.

Past participle
Of regular verbs: The past participle is the same as the past simple. (See page 84.)
Of irregular verbs: See the list of irregular past participles on page 139.

Adverbs used with the present perfect

I've *already* done it./I've done it *already*.
I've done it *before*.
I've *just* done the filing.
With questions: Have you done it *yet*?
                  Have you *ever* been there?
With negatives: I've *never* been there.
                  I haven't seen him *since* 1952.
                  I haven't seen him *for* 20 years.
                  I haven't done it *yet*.

The WILL future

We use the *will* future for a decision made at that moment about the future.
(See page 127 for more notes on the future.)

I He They	will do it tomorrow.	(I'll) (He'll) (They'll)

Negative: I will not do it.   (I won't)

Possessive pronouns

This is	my office. your office. his office. her office. its box. our office. their office.	Whose is it?	It's mine. yours. his. hers. (its.) ours. theirs.

Capital letters

for:	eg:
names and initials	Lorenzo Magnani, J Bradley, SY/JB
titles	Mr, Miss
companies	Brighter Office Supplies Ltd, BOS Ltd, Milgrom & Co
countries, nationalities	Egypt, Italy, English, French
towns, places, rivers, mountains etc.	London, Middlesex, River Thames, Mount Everest
days, months	Monday, Wednesday, January, December
at the beginning of a sentence	Thank you for your letter.
I	I know him and I like him.

Some uses of punctuation marks

Full stop (.)	eg:
At the end of a sentence	He works in Harlow.
In decimals	475.6
In amounts of money	£27.56, $7.25
Question mark (?)	
After a question	Did you see him yesterday?
Comma (,)	
Before and/or after someone's name when you are talking to them	Hello, Helen. Mary, what are you doing?
In a list of several things	She has got long, dark, curly hair. I went to Rome, London and Paris. We need paper, files, rulers and pens. Five people can type, four people cannot type and two people can type a bit.
In numbers over 999	1,650
Before the conjunction *but*	I need some pencils, but I do not need any files.
Before direct speech	He said, 'Hello'.
Apostrophe (')	
Belonging to Mary	Mary's boss
BOS	BOS's staff (or BOS' staff)
the accountant	the accountant's books
the accountants	the accountants' books
Short forms (contractions)	it's (it is/it has), I'll (I will) he won't (he will not), I'm (I am)
Inverted commas/quotation marks	
With direct speech	He says, 'She likes coffee'.
NB Not with reported speech	He said she liked coffee.

Unit Twelve
BOS is the best

 Simon is having lunch in a café near work.

1 Excuse me. Is this seat free?

Yes. Help yourself.

2 I've seen you here before, haven't I?

Probably. I work for a big company near here.

3 Oh, do you? I work for the biggest company in the area. My company sells goods all over Britain.

So does mine.

We make the best office equipment in Britain. 4

No. WE make the best office equipment in Britain.

5 Who do you work for?

Brighter Office Supplies.

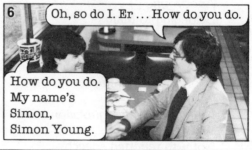

6 Oh, so do I. Er ... How do you do.

How do you do. My name's Simon, Simon Young.

Exercise 182

1 Did Simon know the man in the café?
2 Does the man work near the café?
3 What does the man's company make?

4 Who does the man work for?
5 Who works for the biggest office supply company in the area?

Comparison

Exercise 183

Write the comparative and superlative of these adjectives, like this:
  small – *smaller* – *the smallest*
  expensive – *more expensive* – *the most expensive*

1 cheap 2 efficient 3 heavy 4 wide 5 easy
6 quiet 7 dirty 8 thin 9 big 10 dark 11 tall
12 clean 13 intelligent 14 attractive 15 long 16 noisy

Laboratory drill A
P: This computer is very small.   R: *Mine's smaller.*
P: His calculator is very expensive.   R: *Mine's more expensive.*

Laboratory drill B
P: These computers are very small.   R: *Mine's the smallest.*
P: Their calculators are very expensive. R: *Mine's the most expensive.*

Exercise 184

Look at these pieces of paper. This is not their real size, but they are drawn to scale. They are standard sizes used in offices in Britain. (NB Standard paper sizes have different names in America.)

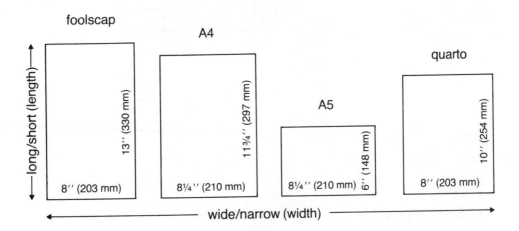

Compare the sheets of paper like this:
A: *Is A4 longer than quarto?*   B: *Yes it is.*
A: *Is foolscap wider than A4?*   B: *No it isn't. A4's wider than foolscap.*
                                           or *Foolscap's narrower than A4.*

A: *Is A5 wider than A4?*   B: *No. They're the same width.*

Laboratory drill A
P: Is A4 longer than quarto?   R: *Yes it is.*
P: Is foolscap wider than quarto?   R: *No it isn't.*

Laboratory drill B
P: Foolscap and A4   R: *Foolscap is longer and narrower than A4.*
                      or Foolscap is narrower and longer
                      than A4.
P: A5 and A4   R: *A5 is shorter than A4.*

Exercise 185   *Word puzzle*

At the side of Simon's and Anne's typewriters are lists of adjectives to describe
them. The adjectives describing Simon's typewriter are the opposites of those
describing Anne's. The adjectives are all hidden in the word puzzle. You can find
them horizontally, vertically and diagonally.

D	I	F	F	I	C	U	L	T
E	A	B	O	D	C	D	I	H
C	X	E	U	B	I	G	G	E
L	U	P	I	M	E	R	H	A
E	S	F	E	A	G	A	I	V
A	E	H	T	N	O	I	S	Y
N	E	W	I	U	S	L	J	Y
K	C	H	E	A	P	I	D	L
S	M	A	L	L	T	O	V	E
E	L	E	C	T	R	I	C	E

Simon's typewriter   Anne's typewriter

expensive   cheap
small   big
light   heavy
electric   manual
c____   d____
quick   noisy
easy to use   difficult to use
new   old

Exercise 186

In pairs, compare the two typewriters, like this:

SIMON: *My typewriter's small.*
ANNE: *You're right. It's smaller than mine.*
ANNE: *My typewriter's difficult to use.*
SIMON: *You're right. It's more difficult to use than mine.*

NB You cannot compare two of the adjectives!

Laboratory drill
P: My typewriter's big.
P: My typewriter's difficult to use.

R: *You're right. It's bigger than mine.*
R: *You're right. It's more difficult to use than mine.*

Exercise 187
Look at Helen's typewriter.

In pairs, compare all three typewriters, like this:
A: *Whose typewriter is the oldest?*   B: *Helen's.*

Laboratory drill
P: Old

R: *Whose typewriter is the oldest?*

Exercise 188   *Reprographics*

Look at these pictures. Helen and Mary have both copied 200 advertising circulars. Helen used a spirit duplicator and Mary used a photocopier. How many comparisons can you make between using a spirit duplicator and using a photocopier?

COST: £   COST: £££

Comparing jobs

Exercise 189

 Listen to the tape. Richard and Penelope are brother and sister. They are talking about their jobs and about Susan's job. Susan is their sister. Fill in a copy of this table with the information on the tape.

	training	hours per week	salary pa	holidays pa
Penelope				3 weeks
Richard	1 year		£4,500	
Susan		20-30		

Question: Who is the youngest in the family?

Exercise 190

Make eight true sentences from this table about Penelope, Richard and Susan.
eg *Penelope earns less money than Richard.*

Penelope Richard Susan	had earns has works	more less fewer longer shorter	holidays training money hours per week	than	Penelope. Richard. Susan.

Exercise 191

Make eight true sentences about Penelope, Richard and Susan, like this:
. . . *had the longest training.*
. . . *works the fewest hours per week.*

Exercise 192   *A survey*

Write down the following true or imaginary details about yourself on a sheet of paper:

Age: . . . .
Length of training: . . . .
Number of hours worked per week: . . . .
Salary: . . . .

Do not show your list to anyone else. Talk to everyone else in the class and find out who is the oldest/youngest, who had the longest/shortest training, etc.

The Guinness Book of Records contains many interesting facts, for example:

Money:
The smallest coins were the Nepalese ¼ dam, called a Jawa. They were made of silver in about 1740. They weighed about 0.008g. The heaviest coin was a Swedish 10 daler in 1644. It weighed 19,710kg.

Typing:
The person who typed for the longest time on an electric typewriter was Gisela Martin of Elgerhausen, W. Germany. She typed for 216 hrs from 19th to 28th July 1980. Mike Howell, a blind office worker from Manchester, holds the record for typing on a manual typewriter. He typed for 120 hrs 15 mins from 25th to 30th November 1969 in Liverpool.
The fastest typists are Margaret Owen from the USA, who typed 170 wpm in one minute on 21st October 1918, and Albert Tangora, also from the USA, who typed at 147 wpm for an hour on 22nd October 1923. These speeds were on manual typewriters.

Salaries:
David Tendler earned the highest recorded salary in the world in 1979 in the USA. The total amount of money he received that year was $2,202,938 (then £1,015,000).

Shorthand:
The fastest recorded shorthand speeds are 300 wpm for 5 mins and 350 wpm for 2 mins. The holder of this record is Nathan Behrin. These speeds were recorded in New York in December 1922.

Working Week:
Young doctors probably have the longest working week. Sometimes they work 139 hours per week which gives them 4 hrs 8½ mins sleep per night. The shortest working week is probably 3 hours. Some university lecturers have a working week of 3 hours which they work for only 24 weeks per year so they work a 72-hour year.

Exercise 193

These are the answers to questions about the passage. Write the questions:
eg 19,710 kg. – *How much did a Swedish 10 daler weigh?*

1 About 0.008 grams
2 A Swedish 10 daler
3 216 hours
4 Mike Howell
5 Margaret Owen and Albert Tangora
6 David Tendler
7 300 wpm for 5 mins and 350 wpm for 2 mins
8 Nathan Behrin
9 Young doctors
10 Three hours

Exercise 194   *Abbreviations*

What are the abbreviations for these words?
1 hour(s)-hr (hrs)
2 kilogram(s)
3 minute(s)
4 gram(s)
5 per annum
6 words per minute

Ask and answer questions, like this:
A: *What does h – r – s stand for?*   B: *Hours.*

Can you think of any more abbreviations? What do they stand for?

Unit 12

Exercise 195   *Comparing situations*

Mary and Helen are comparing their situations with Anne's. Mary's situation is the same as Anne's, but Helen's is different. Fill in the rest on a copy of this table with Mary's and Helen's comments.

ANNE	MARY	HELEN
1 I can type very well.	So can I.	I can't.
2 I've got a lot of work to do.	So have I.	I haven't.
3 I'm very efficient.		
4 I earn a good salary.		
5 I've typed a lot of letters this week.		
6 I photocopied 6 reports yesterday.		
7 I was top of my class at school.		
8 I went to a good secretarial college.		
9 I'm going out for lunch.		
10 I can drive.		

Laboratory drill A
P: I can type very well.   R: *So can I.*
P: I've got a lot of work to do.   R: *So have I.*

Laboratory drill B
P: I can type very well.   R: *I can't.*
P: I've got a lot of work to do.   R: *I haven't.*

Exercise 196   *Advertising circulars*

Advertisers often send letters to customers describing their product. These letters are called advertising circulars. Write three different advertising circulars from the table on the next page.

Dear Customer,

I	are	writing to tell you about our	newest	car.
We	am		latest	soap powder.
			most recent	cooker.

It is probably the	best	you can buy. It is also	cheaper
	most exciting		cleaner
	fastest		more economical
	most reliable		more efficient

than any other	make.	It makes your	coloured	journeys
	model.		short	washing
	brand.		cakes and	tarts

brighter	and your	white	journeys	shorter.
lighter		long	food	whiter.
more enjoyable		fried	washing	crispier.

We	enclose a	sample	for you to	look at.	We	look forward to
I		brochure		try.	I	

hearing from you when you have	used	it.
	read	

For	the name of your nearest supplier	or further information, please	ring	John
	a test drive		contact	
	a demonstration		write to	Mary

Jones	at	01-459 4114 or 01-459 4686.
Smith	on	Smith & Co, 57 Westgate Road, London SW1B 7XY.

Language notes

Comparative and superlative of adjectives

Short words

	comparative		superlative	
small	+ er	= smaller	+ est	= the smallest
wide	+ r	= wider	+ st	= the widest
heavy	+ ier	= heavier	+ iest	= the heaviest

NB   short vowel + consonant ending

big	+ g + er	= bigger	+ g + est	= the biggest

Long words

intelligent	more intelligent	the most intelligent
expensive	more expensive	the most expensive

Some irregular adjectives

good	better	the best
bad	worse	the worst

Also:

Some, many, a lot of, much	more	the most
a little (with mass nouns)	less	the least
a few (with count nouns)	fewer	the fewest

Unit Thirteen
Complaints

Paul Johnson is showing some office furniture to a customer.

So you'd like to buy a filing cabinet? Well, ours are very popular.

They're made in this country and...
What about delivery?

Er... they're sent straight from our warehouse and delivered free.
And are they packed securely?

Yes of course they are.

Because I ordered some furniture from you last year and it was damaged. A chair seat was torn, a typewriter was dented and a desk handle was broken.

Ah... Sorry.

Exercise 197

1 Do many people like BOS filing cabinets?
2 How much does delivery cost?
3 Was anything wrong with this customer's last order from BOS?
4 Which was damaged most, the chair, the typewriter or the desk?

Unit 13

Exercise 198   *What's wrong?*

There is something wrong with these objects. In pairs, use the verbs below
to discuss them, like this:

A: *What's wrong with the*
    paper? (What is wrong . . .?)   B: *It's torn.* (It is torn.)
A: *What's wrong with the*
    cheque?   B: *It's not signed.*

tear – sign – dent – finish – break – crack

chair   paper   plate

letter   car   cheque

> *Laboratory drill*
> P: What's wrong with the paper?   R: *It's torn.*
> P: What's wrong with the cheque?   R: *It's not signed.*

Exercise 199   *A speech*

Look back at the notes for Fred McLean's speech in Exercise 170. Write the
sentences in the passive, like this:
Last May a branch was opened in Liverpool.

> *Laboratory drill*
> P: We opened a branch in Liverpool last May.
> R: *Last May a branch was opened in Liverpool.*

Numbers revision

Exercise 200

The figures in the number 6,590 can be mixed up to make other numbers,
like this: 6,950; 6,059; 5,906 etc

Make as many other numbers as you can using these figures and write them out
in words, like this:
6,950   *six thousand, nine hundred and fifty.*
9,506   *nine thousand, five hundred and six.*

Do the same with these figures: 7,211 – 4,444 – 8,030

> *Laboratory drill*
> P: Six five nine oh   R: *Six thousand, five hundred and ninety*

Exercise 201

Notice how we say these calculations:

$3+1=4$ *Three plus one equals four.*
$4-1=3$ *Four minus one equals three.*
$2 \times 4=8$ *Two times four equals eight.*
$6 \div 3=2$ *Six divided by three equals two.*

Listen to the tape and write down the answers to the simple calculations you hear, eg Number 1: *6*

Laboratory drill	
P: Two four eight	R: *Two times four equals eight.*
P: Nine three three	R: *Nine divided by three equals three.*

Post room procedures

Exercise 202

Simon is talking to George in the post room about a missing memo. Listen to the tape and write down which word belongs to which number in the diagram about post room procedures.

business – personal or confidential – first class letters –
second class letters – parcels – internal post –
delivered – distributed – franked – labelled – opened – collected – sorted –
sorted – weighed – weighed if necessary – wrapped

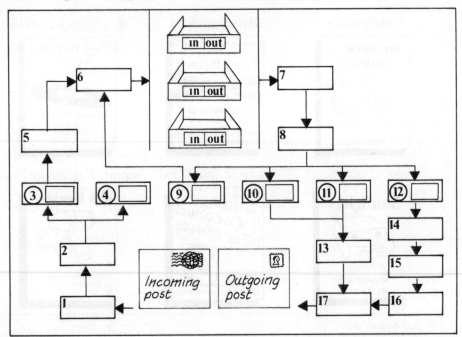

Question: What happened to Simon's memo?

Exercise 203

Choose the correct word in each bracket and write two paragraphs about post room procedures.

The incoming post is 1 (*collected/distributed/delivered*) by the 2 (*postman/post room*) at about 9 o'clock every morning. In the 3 (*post room/postbox*) the post is 4 (*delivered/sorted/distributed*) into two categories: business letters and personal or confidential letters. The 5 (*business/personal/confidential*) letters are opened and all the post is 6 (*collected/distributed*) to the different departments. In the afternoon the outgoing post is 7 (*collected/sorted/distributed*) from each department and it is 8 (*collected/sorted/distributed*) into four categories: internal post, first class letters, second class letters and parcels. The 9 (*first class letters/second class letters/parcels*) are wrapped, labelled and weighed, and the 10 (*letters/parcels*) are weighed if necessary. All the 11 (*parcels/letters/post*) is then franked with the correct postage and taken to the 12 (*postbox/postman/ post room*). The 13 (*outgoing post/internal post/first class post*) is distributed the next morning with the incoming post.

Laboratory drill
P: The postman delivers the incoming post.   R: *The incoming post is delivered.*
P: Someone sorts the post into two categories.   R: *The post is sorted into two categories.*

Exercise 204   *Advertisements*

Use the verbs under the pictures to ask and answer questions, like this:
A: *Who is 'We Mean Business' written by?*   B: *Susan Norman.*
A: *What are the blouses made of?*   B: *Silk.*

write/publish   direct/produce   sing/arrange/conduct

make (2 questions)   make (2 questions)   import (2 questions)/make

Laboratory drill
P: Who is 'We Mean Business' written by?   R: *Susan Norman*

Exercise 205   *World exports*

Look at the map and decide which export you associate with which country.

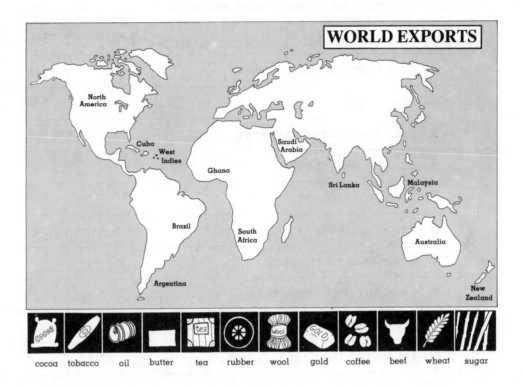

In pairs, discuss the exports, like this:

A: *Where is coffee grown?*   B: *In Brazil.*
A: *Where is coffee exported from?*   B: *Brazil.*

Use these verbs:
coffee/tea/sugar/wheat   – *grow (in)*
rubber/beef/butter   – *produce (in)*
gold   – *mine (in)*
wool/oil/tobacco   – *export (from)*

Laboratory drill
P: Brazil exports coffee.   R: *Coffee is exported from Brazil.*
P: They grow coffee in Brazil.   R: *Coffee is grown in Brazil.*

Exercise 206   *Project*

Go round different shops and find out what goods your country imports from
other countries. Write a short report about your research.

Unit 13

Exercise 207   *Comparing situations*

Mary and Helen are comparing their situation with Anne's. Mary's situation is the same as Anne's, but Helen's is different. Fill in a copy of this table with Mary and Helen's comments on Anne's negative statements.

ANNE	MARY	HELEN
1 I don't like using the telephone.	*Nor do I.*	*I do.*
2 I can't swim.	*Nor can I.*	*I can.*
3 I didn't go to work on Monday.		
4 I haven't been to Egypt.		
5 I don't cycle to work.		
6 I'm not going out to lunch today.		
7 I wasn't given a pay rise.		
8 I wouldn't like to leave BOS.		
9 I haven't got any more holiday this year.		
10 I'm not very busy.		

Laboratory drill A
P: I don't like using the telephone.   R: *Nor do I.*
P: I can't swim.   R: *Nor can I.*

Laboratory drill B
P: I don't like using the telephone.   R: *I do.*
P: I can't swim.   R: *I can.*

Exercise 208   *Telexes*

Telex messages must be very short. Many words used in ordinary sentences are shortened or left out of telex messages. Look at these sentences:

I would be grateful if you could send me . . . PLEASE SEND . . .

I am afraid that order 62035 was damaged REGRET ORDER 62035 DAMAGED

I am coming on Friday at 6.30 COMING FRIDAY 1830

This is to confirm that our agent is arriving . . . CONFIRM AGENT ARRIVING

112

Here are some sentences from letters. Write them as they are written in a telex.

1 I would be grateful if you could send us 20 filing cabinets, type SD52.
2 I confirm that our agent is arriving at Gatwick airport on Saturday 22nd August.
3 I would be grateful if you could confirm the despatch of order 520.
4 I am afraid that order 665 was delayed at the customs.
5 Mr Smith is arriving at Waterloo at 3.30 pm. I would be grateful if you could meet him.
6 I am afraid that four typewriters in order 0039 were damaged. Our agents are investigating the matter. I would be grateful if you could send immediate replacements.
7 I am arriving at Victoria at 5 pm. I would be grateful if you could meet me.
8 I would be grateful if you could confirm the arrival of order 6290.
9 I would be grateful if you could confirm that your agent is arriving at Heathrow airport on Tuesday.
10 I have received your order 87654.

Exercise 209   *Letter of complaint*

This is the telex that the customer on page 107 sent to BOS when he received the damaged order on 19th October 1981:
ORDER 98534 ARRIVED DAMAGED CHAIR SEAT TORN DESK HANDLE BROKEN TYPEWRITER DENTED PLEASE SEND IMMEDIATE REPLACEMENTS

Write this information in the form of a letter of complaint to Sheila Baker. The customer is Sam Worthington, the manager of Worthington Ltd, 5 Milton Street, Polegate, Sussex LW3 5DR.

Language notes

The passive

to be (all tenses) + past participle
eg: Coffee is grown in Brazil. (Coffee's)
    The letters are collected in the afternoon.
    This book was written by Susan Norman.
    The letters were sorted into three categories.

Question
Was the chair broken?
Where are they made?
Coffee's exported from Brazil, isn't it?
Negative
They aren't (They're not) made in this country.
The chair wasn't broken.

Short answers
Yes it was. No it wasn't.

Past participles

Of regular verbs: The past participle is the same as the past simple.
Of irregular verbs: See the list of irregular verbs on page 139.

Unit Fourteen
Telephone messages

 Fred is in his office. His telephone is ringing. Mary is in the next room.

1 That sounds like Fred's personal phone ringing.

2 Do you want me to answer the phone?

3 Yes please, Mary. It might be the bank manager. I don't want to talk to him.

4 But I'm also waiting for a call from the garage about my car.

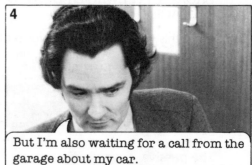

5 And it might be my wife. I want to talk to her.

Yes, Mr McLean.

Oh. It's too late. It's stopped ringing.

6

Exercise 210

1 Whose phone is ringing?
2 Who doesn't Fred want to talk to?
3 Who does Fred want to talk to?
4 Why doesn't Mary answer the phone?

Exercise 211   *Look like . . .*

Look at these pictures. They are all things you find in an office. What do you
think they are? Talk about them like this:

It could be   *a . . .*
It might be   *part of a . . .*
It looks like

Turn to the next page for the correct answers.

Laboratory drill A P: A typewriter	R: *It could be a typewriter.*
Laboratory drill B P: A typewriter	R: *It might be part of a typewriter.*
Laboratory drill C P: A typewriter	R: *It looks like part of a typewriter.*

Exercise 212   *Answers to exercise 211*

These are pictures of the same things you saw on page 115. Talk about them
like this:
It didn't look like a . . ., but it was.
It looked like part of a . . ., but it wasn't.

> *Laboratory drill*
> P: A typewriter   R: *It didn't look like a typewriter, but it was.*

Exercise 213   *Too early*

Look at these pictures. What do you think each person is saying? These are the
adjectives they are using: *big – dangerous – early – expensive – late – long –
short – small*

> *Laboratory drill*
> P: Picture 1. Early   R: *We're too early.*

116

Exercise 214   *It doesn't fit*

In the last four pictures BOS staff are buying clothes. The clothes do not fit.
Have conversations with the shop assistant as the BOS staff do:

ASSISTANT: *What a lovely coat!*
MARY: *I think it's too big.*
ASSISTANT: *But you look very nice in it.*
MARY: { *Oh all right. I'll take it.*
                      { *I'm sorry. I don't want it.*

Laboratory drill A
First take Mary's part and then take the assistant's part in the dialogue. Mary buys the coat.

Laboratory drill B
First take Helen's part and then take the assistant's part in the dialogue. Helen doesn't buy the dress.

Laboratory drill C
First take Howard's part and then take the assistant's part in the dialogue. Howard buys the jacket.

Laboratory drill D
First take Simon's part and then take the assistant's part in the dialogue. Simon doesn't buy the trousers.

Homophones

Exercise 215

A homophone is a word which sounds exactly the same as another word but which is spelt differently and has a different meaning
eg   *meet – meat*

Make a list of the homophones for these words. You can find them hidden vertically, horizontally and diagonally in this word puzzle.

right	sea
there	weight
know	here
won	red
too	weigh

N	T	W	O	N	E
W	O	R	S	H	W
A	A	I	E	E	A
I	B	T	E	A	Y
T	H	E	I	R	D

Exercise 216

Listen to these sentences on the tape and fill in the missing words. Be careful with the spelling.

1 Turn . . . at the corner.
2 Mary . . . the Ideal Secretary competition.
3 I can't . . . you.
4 I don't . . . the answer.
5 I'm going . . .
6 Can you . . . the . . .?
7 That's a lovely . . . dress.
8 Can you . . . these parcels please?
9 . . . a moment please.
10 It's over . . .
11 Have you . . . this report?
12 I thought it was . . .
13 Please . . . a letter to Mr Sawyers.
14 Have you got a bigger . . . please?
15 Am I going the . . . . . .?
16 Give them . . . coats.
17 This is . . . difficult.
18 . . ., . . ., three.

Reported speech

Exercise 217

Mary is answering Fred's phone because Fred is very busy. Mary tells him what the person on the phone says and tells the person on the phone what he says, like this:

FRED: *What does she say?*   MARY: *She says she's your wife.*
WIFE: *What does he say?*   MARY: *He says he's leaving in half an hour.*

NB   The verb 'say' is in the present tense, so the tense of the reported speech does not change.

1 I'm his wife.

2 I'm leaving work in half an hour.

3 It's urgent.

4 I'll ring her back.

5 He can't ring me back. I'm in a phone box.

6 I'm very busy.

7 The football match starts in 15 minutes.

8 I'll leave immediately.

Laboratory drill
P: I'm his wife.
P: I'm leaving work in half an hour.

R: *She says she's your wife.*
R: *He says he's leaving work in half an hour.*

Exercise 218

Mary is telling Helen about the conversation on the phone yesterday, like this:

HELEN: *What did she say?*   MARY: *She said she was his wife.*

HELEN: *What did he say?*   MARY: *He said he was leaving work in half an hour.*

NB   The verb 'said' is in the past tense, so the reported speech is in the past too.

present simple ⟶ past simple
will   ⟶   would
can   ⟶   could

Laboratory drill
P: I'm his wife.   R: *She said she was his wife.*
P: I'm leaving work in half an hour. R: *He said he was leaving work in half an hour.*

Telephone messages

Exercise 219

Look at this message and answer the questions:

1 Who rang?
2 Who is the message for?
3 Who answered the phone?
4 What time was the telephone call?
5 Where does Mr Cox work?

6   What does Mr Cox want to do?
7   What does he want Sheila to do?
8   Is the message important?
9   What is Mr Cox's number?
10 Did Mr Cox come to the office?

Laboratory drill
P: I want to speak to Sheila about an order.
R: *He said he wanted to speak to Sheila about an order.*

Unit 14

Exercise 220

 Listen to these three telephone conversations on the tape. Anne answers the phone and the three people she speaks to are:
1 David Rogers of Rogers & Co.
2 Fiona Donaldson of Of-Op Ltd.
3 Adam Haines.

Write the messages Anne took from the three telephone calls on forms like this one:

```
                       MESSAGE FOR
M ..............................
                  WHILE YOU WERE OUT
M ..............................
of ..............................
TEL NO ..............................
```

TELEPHONED		PLEASE RING	
CALLED TO SEE YOU		WILL CALL AGAIN	
WANTS TO SEE YOU		URGENT	

```
MESSAGE: ..............................
..............................................
..............................................
..............................................
..............................................
..............................................
DATE: ..................   TIME: ..............
RECEIVED BY: ..............................
```

Laboratory drill
P: He said he wanted to see her.   R: *I want to see her.*

Exercise 221

Write the telephone conversation you think Anne had with Steven Cox when he rang on 16th December (see Exercise 219).

Exercise 222   *Roleplay*

Act out imaginary telephone conversations between Anne and
1 someone who is phoning to complain that his last order was damaged.
2 someone who is phoning to ask Sheila to a party.
3 someone in the BOS warehouse. Sheila has ordered some stationery, but she has not written the quantities or what sizes she wants.

The person who is Anne can write a message for Sheila. You can then use this message to help you practise the telephone conversations again.

Language notes

Reported speech
(also called indirect speech)

verb of saying	spoken words (direct speech)	reported speech
Present simple eg He says / I think / You know	+ *All tenses* 'She likes coffee' 'He was there' 'They're going to leave'	NO CHANGE He says she likes coffee. I think he was there. You know they're going to leave.
Past simple eg John said	+ *Simple present* 'She likes tea'	*Simple past* John said she liked tea.
eg John said	+ *Tenses with 'to be'* 'She is working' 'They are going to leave.'	*Past tense of verb 'to be'* John said she was working. John said they were going to leave.
	can / must / have to / have got to / will	could / had to / would
NB He said, 'I like coffee.'		He said *he* liked coffee.

We do not use inverted commas with reported speech (see page 97).

Unit Fifteen
Plans

A local newspaper reporter is writing an article about BOS Ltd. Fred has just explained the company's plans.

1 Have you got any questions?

2 Yes, Mr McLean. You said you were going to sell new items of stationery.

3 What exactly are you going to sell?

Well, I'm afraid I haven't got a precise list with me.

4 Mmm. You also said you were going to close your Middlesex branch. When exactly are you going to do that?

5 I don't know the precise date, of course ... er ... Are there any more questions?

6 No thank you, Mr McLean. I think I understand your plans ...

Exercise 223

1 What are BOS going to sell?
2 Which branch are BOS going to close?

3 When are BOS going to close one of their branches?

Daydreams

Exercise 224

Helen does not like being a secretary. She is daydreaming about a better life. Put these notes in the right order and, in pairs, talk about her plans, like this:

A: *I'm going to improve my typing.*   B: *Oh are you?*

improve my typing – marry my boss – travel abroad – have a lot of children – earn more money – do a lot of housework – work for a handsome boss

Laboratory drill
P: Improve my typing

R: *She's going to improve her typing.*

Exercise 225

Helen's daydream went a bit wrong, but she knows what she is not going to do! In pairs, talk about these pictures, like this:

A: *I'm not going to open the post.*   B: *Oh aren't you?*

Laboratory drill
P: Open the post

R: *She's not going to open the post.*

Exercise 226   *Plans*

Interview three people in your class about their plans for the next few years. Their plans can include things they are not going to do. Write a few sentences about each person.

Unit 15

Town planning

Exercise 227   *Town planning*

Listen to the tape. Anne and Simon are talking about future changes in Harlow.
Look at the map and answer the questions:

1 Which road is going to be one-way? a) Maddox Road going north b) Maddox Road going south c) Rose Hill going north d) Rose Hill going south
2 What number is the bus route C – D?
3 Draw a small map and mark the changes to the bus route.
4 Which building are they going to close? a) the post office b) the bank
   c) the station d) the newsagent's
5 What number is the bus route A – B?
6 Which building is going to move? a) the supermarket b) the newsagent's
   c) the post office d) the bank
7 Which letter is where the new supermarket is going to be? I – J – K – L
8 Which letter is where the new cinema is going to be? E – F – G – H
9 Which building are they going to knock down? a) the supermarket b) the cinema
   c) the bank d) the post office
10 Which letter is where the new roundabout is going to be? M – N – O – P

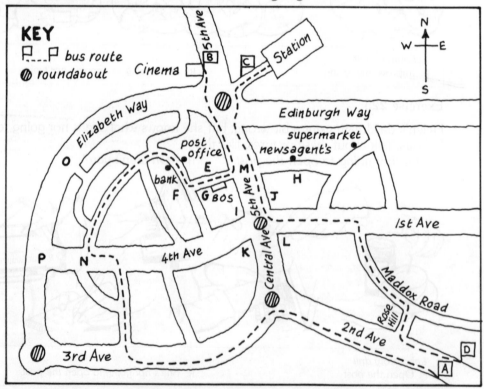

Laboratory drill
P: They're going to make Rose Hill one way.
R: *They're not going to make Rose Hill one way, are they?*
P: The bus route is going to change.
R: *The bus route isn't going to change, is it?*

A meeting

Exercise 228   *Hidden word puzzle*

Read this account of a meeting and then fill in a copy of this word puzzle. The words in the puzzle are all in the passage.

> Fred McLean looked at the agenda to see what the meeting was about. He was in the chair, so he was in charge of the meeting. He looked around. Everybody was present. He opened the meeting at 10 am. Everybody approved the minutes of the last meeting. Then they discussed all the items on the agenda. Mary took the minutes. Fred closed the meeting at 11.45.

Clues

1   The official account of a meeting
2   To begin a meeting
3   A point to discuss
4   Verb meaning to *write* the minutes
5   The person in charge is 'in the . . .'
6   If you are at a meeting you are . . .
7   The list of things to discuss at a meeting
8   To finish a meeting

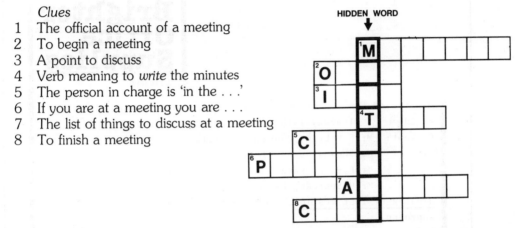

Exercise 229   *The agenda*

This is the agenda for a meeting at BOS. Mary is going to take the minutes. She has marked the agenda with ticks (√) and crosses (×). She thinks she knows what the meeting will decide. In pairs, talk about the meeting like this:

SIMON: *Are they going to approve the minutes of the last meeting?*

MARY: √ *Yes I think so.*
         × *No I don't think so.*

Brighter Office Supplies Limited

Meeting of managers to be held in the managing director's office at 10 am on Tuesday 15th December 1981.

AGENDA
1   Approving the minutes of the last meeting
2   Redecorating the building ✓
3   Enlarging the office space X
4   Expanding the business ✓
5   Hiring more staff ✓
6   Exporting to Italy X
7   Closing the Middlesex branch X
8   Any other business

Laboratory drill A
P: Are they going to approve the minutes of the last meeting?   R: *Yes I think so.*
                                                                   or *No I don't think so.*

Laboratory drill B
P: Approving the minutes of the last meeting   R: *Are they going to approve the minutes of the last meeting?*

Exercise 230 *The minutes*

These are the minutes Mary typed after the meeting. Write *one* suitable word for each gap.

Brighter Office Supplies
Limited

Minutes of the[1]   of managers held in the managing[2]   office at 10 am [3]   Tuesday 15th December 1981.

Present: Mr F McLean, Managing director (in[4]   chair)

Ms Sheila Baker, Sales manager

Mr P Hall, Head of accounts

Mr H Spencer, Personnel manager

Minutes of last meeting. The minutes of the last meeting[5] approved.

Redecorating the building. Mr McLean said the building was being redecorated[6]   January and February. He said it was going[7]   take about a week to decorate each floor. They[8] going to start with the ground[9]   in the second week of January.

Enlarging the office. The managers talked about enlarging the office. Mr Hall said it was too expensive. Ms Baker[10]   it was not necessary to enlarge[11]   office immediately. The managers agreed not to[12]   the office.

Expanding the business and Exporting to Italy. The managers agreed to expand the business. Ms Baker said there was a new market[13]   Italy. She said Lorenzo Magnani would be[14]   charge. (Her report[15]   attached to these minutes.)

Closing the Middlesex branch and Hiring more staff. Mr McLean said they were[16]   the Middlesex[17] . He said it[18]   losing money. Mr Spencer said BOS needed more[19]   at their Harlow main office. Mr McLean said they would offer jobs at Harlow to the Middlesex staff.

There was no further business.

The meeting closed[20]   11.45 am.

Exercise 231   *Reported speech*

There is a lot of reported speech in the minutes. Write what people actually said, like this:

1   Mr McLean said it was going to take a week. *It's going to take a week.*
2   He said they were going to start in January.
3   Mr Hall said it was too expensive.
4   Ms Baker said it was not necessary.
5   Ms Baker said there was a new market in Italy.
6   She said Lorenzo Magnani would be in charge.
7   Mr McLean said they were closing the Middlesex branch.
8   He said it was losing money.
9   Mr Spencer said BOS needed more staff at their Harlow main office.
10   Mr McLean said they would offer jobs at Harlow to the Middlesex staff.

> *Laboratory drill*
> P: Mr McLean said it was going to take a week.   R: *It's going to take a week.*

Exercise 232   *News article*

Look at Fred's interview on page 122 and the agenda and minutes of the meeting in Exercises 229 and 230. Use this information to write a short article for the local newspaper about BOS company plans. .

Language notes

The future

Going to+ infinitive

We use the *going to* future for plans which are not definite:
I'm going to visit my mother soon.
BOS are going to close one of their branches.
When are you going to leave?
Are you going to see him soon?

Present progressive

We use the present progressive future for definite plans and arrangements (we know *when* we are doing things):
I'm seeing him tomorrow.
What are you doing tonight?

Present simple

We use the present simple future about timetables:
The train leaves at 6 o'clock

Will

We use the *will* future for decisions we make at that moment about the future:
Oh, all right. I'll go with you.

Consolidation Unit C
Your news and news extracts

*Your News – the radio programme for you
and* News Extracts – *interesting articles from the newspapers*

Headlines

Exercise 233

The first things you look at in a newspaper are the headlines. The 'grammar' of news headlines is something like the grammar of telexes. Here are some of the 'rules'. Can you arrange these headlines into four groups?

1 *no verbs* (the news story is usually in the present tense)
2 *present simple tense* (the news story is usually in the past tense)
3 *past participle* (the news story is usually in the past tense and/or in the passive)
4 *infinitive* – 'somebody *to do* something' (the news story is usually about the future)

---

a Record Export Figures   c **OFFICE EXPLOSION**

d *Focus on Europe*

b High Street Price War

f **ABC BOSS DIES**   e BOSS STARTS FACTORY FIRE

g PM to return for funeral

h **Bomb planted by secretary**   k Police Investigate Fire

i **BIG PRICE CUTS**

l *Export figures to rise*

j FIRE STARTED BY BOSS

Exercise 234

Look at all the news items on page 129. Which headline is most suitable for which article?

NB   There are more headlines than there are articles.

Exercise 235   *Wrong order*

The lines in article 1 are in the wrong order. Rewrite the article correctly.

Exercise 236 *Missing words*

There is one word missing from each line in article 2 below. What are the missing words? Where are they missing from?

Exercise 237 *Bad printing*

Some of the words in article 3 are badly printed and you cannot read them. Write one word for each word which is badly printed.

Exercise 238 *Reported speech*

Look through the news articles below for examples of reported speech. Write the words people actually said.

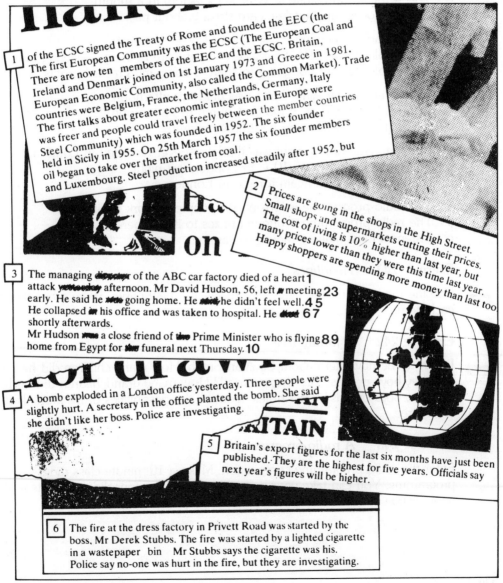

1 of the ECSC signed the Treaty of Rome and founded the EEC (the The first European Community was the ECSC (The European Coal and There are now ten members of the EEC and the ECSC. Britain, Ireland and Denmark joined on 1st January 1973 and Greece in 1981. European Economic Community, also called the Common Market). Trade countries were Belgium, France, the Netherlands, Germany, Italy The first talks about greater economic integration in Europe were was freer and people could travel freely between the member countries Steel Community) which was founded in 1952. The six founder held in Sicily in 1955. On 25th March 1957 the six founder members oil began to take over the market from coal. and Luxembourg. Steel production increased steadily after 1952, but

2 Prices are going in the shops in the High Street. Small shops and supermarkets cutting their prices. The cost of living is 10% higher than last year, but many prices lower than they were this time last year. Happy shoppers are spending more money than last too

3 The managing director of the ABC car factory died of a heart **1** attack yesterday afternoon. Mr David Hudson, 56, left meeting **23** early. He said he was going home. He said he didn't feel well. **45** He collapsed in his office and was taken to hospital. He died **67** shortly afterwards. Mr Hudson was a close friend of the Prime Minister who is flying **89** home from Egypt for the funeral next Thursday. **10**

4 A bomb exploded in a London office yesterday. Three people were slightly hurt. A secretary in the office planted the bomb. She said she didn't like her boss. Police are investigating.

5 Britain's export figures for the last six months have just been published. They are the highest for five years. Officials say next year's figures will be higher.

6 The fire at the dress factory in Privett Road was started by the boss, Mr Derek Stubbs. The fire was started by a lighted cigarette in a wastepaper bin Mr Stubbs says the cigarette was his. Police say no-one was hurt in the fire, but they are investigating.

Consolidation Unit C

Exercise 239   *News quiz*

Make up a news quiz. Write one question about each article on page 129. Give your questions to someone else in the class to answer. Answer the questions you are given.

Exercise 240   *Radio news*

Listen to the news on the tape. Decide which is the *most important* point in each news item.

NB   All the statements are true.

1 a There is a strike at Whitaker's biscuit factory.
    b This is the second strike at Whitaker's factory in a month.
    c The employees at Whitaker's are striking about pay.

2 a An insurance company made a record profit last year.
    b The employees of FPA insurance company are holding a meeting tonight.
    c The employees are not going to share a company's record profits.

3 a The funeral of Sir Alan Smith was held this afternoon.
    b A funeral was held at St Mary's Church this afternoon.
    c Sir Alan was married and had three children.

4 a The temperature last night was the lowest ever recorded in London.
    b The temperature was $-10°C$ in London last night.
    c It's going to be cold again tonight in London.

5 a The radio programme is looking for people to work for it.
    b The radio programme is offering prizes to its listeners.
    c Listeners must make a radio programme.

Exercise 241   *Headlines*

Imagine the items on the news are articles in a newspaper. Write a headline for each item.

Exercise 242   *A family tree*

Listen to the news item about Sir Alan Smith. How many children did he have? Are they boys or girls? Are they married? How many grandchildren did he have? Are they boys or girls? Write notes about all the possibilities of his immediate family tree.

Exercise 243   *A radio programme*

Enter the radio programme competition. Make a 10-minute class radio programme. You can take your news items from the consolidation units in this book or you can make up your own.

Tapescript

Unit One

Exercise 3

The editor of the BOS magazine is talking to Howard Spencer.

HS: I'm Howard Spencer. How do you do.

ED: How do you do, Mr Spencer. I'm the new editor of the BOS magazine and I'm writing an article about the BOS staff at head office. I want to tell the sales representatives abroad about you.

HS: Oh yes.

ED: I wonder if you could give me some information?

HS: Yes certainly. What do you want to know?

ED: Well, firstly . . . what does Fred McLean do?

HS: He's the managing director.

ED: Oh I see. Fred McLean is the managing director. And what about Luisa Middle?

HS: Luisa's the receptionist.

ED: Luisa Middle is the receptionist. Good. Is Simon Young a sales assistant?

HS: Yes he is.

ED: Simon Young's a sales assistant. Who's the sales manager?

HS: That's Sheila Baker.

ED: Right. Sheila Baker is the sales manager.

HS: Who's next on your list?

ED: Mary Mackie.

HS: She's a secretary. She's Fred McLean's personal secretary.

ED: Mary Mackie's a personal secretary. Is Paul Johnson a secretary too?

HS: No he isn't. He's a sales rep. – A sales representative.

ED: Paul Johnson's a sales representative. And what does Joy Bradley do?

HS: Joy Bradley's a secretary. She's the secretary in the sales department.

ED: Secretary. Right. Well that's all. Thank you very much.

HS: Wait a minute. You've forgotten me.

ED: Oh yes. Howard Spencer. You're the personnel manager, aren't you?

HS: Yes. That's right.

ED: Howard Spencer . . . the personnel manager. Right then. Thank you very much, Mr Spencer.

Exercise 10

Two guests are registering at a hotel in Harlow. The hotel receptionist is asking them for information.

REC: What's your name please?

PD: Dupont.

REC: How do you spell that?

PD: D-U-P-O-N-T. Dupont.

REC: D-U-P-O-N-T. And your first name, Mr Dupont?

PD: Paul.

REC: What nationality are you?

PD: I'm French.

REC: And what is your occupation?

PD: I'm a representative of Brighter Office Supplies Ltd.

REC: Thank you, Mr Dupont. Could you sign here please?

REC: Good evening. Could you tell me your name please?

MS: Mary Simmons.

REC: First name – Mary. Can you spell your surname?

MS: S-I- double M-O-N-S. Simmons.

REC: You're American, aren't you?

MS: Yes I am.

REC: And your occupation?

MS: I'm a secretary with The London Company.

REC: A secretary – The London Company. Thank you, Miss Simmons. Would you sign here please?

Unit Two

Exercise 19

Write down the number you hear in each sentence. Write down the number only. There are fifteen sentences.
Example.

Sentence 1:   It's twelve o'clock.
You write down – twelve.

S.1: It's *twelve* o'clock. (12)

S.2: The Financial Times index rose by *three* points yesterday. (3)

S.3: I paid *nineteen* dollars for it. (19)

S.4: You want the number *eighteen* bus. (18)

S.5: He's *eleven* years old next week. (11)

S.6: That'll be *fifteen* pence please. (15)

S.7: The speed limit's *ten* miles per hour. (10)

S.8: It's about your order number *oh nine four*. (094)

S.9: My telephone number's *seven eight six, four two one four*. That's 786 4214

S.10: It's *sixteen* centimetres long. (16)

S.11: I want *five* metres of material. (5)

S.12: *Two* pints of milk today please. (2)

S.13: We'll give you a discount of *thirteen* per cent. (13)

S.14: Isn't that a *twenty* pound note? (20)

S.15: I'll be on holiday for *a* month. (1)

131

Tapescript

Exercise 23

A business school teacher is explaining the parts of a business letter to a student.

T: Well then, your company's name and address is printed at the top of the letter. This is called the letterhead.
S: I see. So the letterhead's at the top of the letter.
T: Yes. And the person you are writing to is the reader.
S: And the reader's name and address is on the left.
T: That's right. Below the reader's name and address are the references.
S: Oh yes. 'Ref' is short for 'reference', I suppose.
T: Yes. The references are usually the initials of the writer's name and the initials of the secretary's name. In this letter JB stands for Joy Bradley and SY stands for Simon Young.
S: Oh I see.
T: Now, what is there on the right?
S: The twenty-third of January, nineteen eighty one. Oh. It's the date.
T: Yes. The date's on the right. Now, on the left, under the references is the opening salutation.
S: The opening salutation. Is that 'Dear Ms Meiners'?
T: Yes. And below the opening salutation is the body of the letter – this is what you really want to write.
S: So the body of the letter is between the opening salutation and the closing salutation.
T: Yes. 'Yours sincerely' is the closing salutation.
S: And then there is the signature and the writer's name and the writer's position in the firm.
T: That's right. The signature is above the writer's name and the name is above the writer's position in the firm. What's Simon Young's position?
S: He's a sales assistant.
T: Right.
S: What does 'Encl' mean at the bottom?
T: It stands for 'enclosure'. It means something is enclosed with the letter.
S: Oh I see. In this letter the enclosure is the catalogue.
T: Right.

Unit Three

Exercise 30

Two people are talking about what the BOS staff are doing.

A: Are the staff of BOS very busy?
B: Oh yes. They're always busy.
A: What are they doing now, for example?
B: Well, Luisa's in reception. She's welcoming a visitor at the moment and Anne's in her office. She's typing a letter.
A: Where's Howard Spencer?
B: He's in his office. He's interviewing someone. And Joy's taking shorthand. She's in Sheila's office.
A: They do sound busy. You're right. But Fred isn't in his office.
B: No. He's visiting a customer today.
A: And what's Simon doing?
B: He's talking on the phone.
A: I see. And Mary?
B: She's sending a telex.
A: What about Helen and Paul? What are they doing?
B: Er . . . Well, er . . . Helen's reading a magazine and Paul's having lunch.
A: Reading a magazine and having lunch. They're not very busy, are they?

Exercise 35

Write down the ordinal number you hear in each sentence. Write down the number only. There are ten sentences.

S.1: Jones Company Limited is on the *seventh* floor. (7th)
S.2: My birthday's on the *thirteenth* of January. (13th)
S.3: That's the *third* time I've told you. (3rd)
S.4: He's the *first* person to be sacked. (1st)
S.5: Take the *fourth* road on the right. (4th)
S.6: She won *second* prize in the secretarial competition. (2nd)
S.7: She's the *ninth* person I've interviewed this morning. (9th)
S.8: I'll see you on the *fifteenth* of August. (15th)
S.9: I think it's the *sixth* door on the left. (6th)
S.10: King Henry the *eighth* had six wives. (8th)

Unit Four

Exercise 46

Listen to Joy talking about her routine:

JOY: Right, Anne. The routine's very simple. I start work at half past nine and the first thing I do is open the post – that's at about 9.35. Then I go into Sheila's office at about ten o'clock to take shorthand for an hour. After that we have a coffee break. I make coffee at about eleven o'clock. Then I start typing letters at about 11.30. I have lunch at about half past one, but I only have an hour for lunch, so I'm back in the office by 2.30. I usually go to the telex room at about twenty-five to three and I make tea at four o'clock. I start doing the filing at about 4.30 and I leave the office to go home at 5.30 on the dot.

132

Unit Five

Exercise 65

Write down the number referred to in each sentence. Write down the number only.

S.1: It's *midnight*. (12)
S.2: I need *a couple* of sheets of paper please. (2)
S.3: Can I have a *dozen* please? (12)
S.4: Have you got a *twelve*-inch ruler please? (12)
S.5: It's *ten forty-five* exactly. (10.45)
S.6: How many is *half a dozen*? (6)
S.7: It's *noon*. (12)
S.8: This is the *eighth* sentence. (8)
S.9: I've got *two dozen* pencils. (24)
S.10: I haven't got *any* paper. (0)

Exercise 72

Charlie Alexander is talking to Janet Elvin at the warehouse. He's ordering some stationery.

CA: Hello. Is that the BOS warehouse?
JE: Yes. Can I help you?
CA: This is Charlie Alexander from BOS head office. We need some stationery rather urgently.
JE: What's your order number please?
CA: Six four nine two.
JE: Six four nine two. All right. What do you need?
CA: Firstly . . . eighty reams of quarto typing paper.
JE: Eighty reams of quarto typing paper.
CA: Two hundred files.
JE: Two hundred files. Quarto or A4?
CA: A4.
JE: Two hundred A4 files. Uh-huh. Next?
CA: Six dozen twelve-inch rulers.
JE: The long ones. Right. Seventy-two twelve-inch rulers.
CA: And we also need sixty rolls of one-inch sellotape.
JE: Just a minute. Can you say that again please?
CA: Sixty rolls of one-inch sellotape. That's the wide sellotape.
JE: Yes. I've got that. Anything else?
CA: Yes. Fifty boxes of paper clips. Oh . . . that's small paper clips.
JE: Fifty boxes of small paper clips.
CA: And we need some ballpoints. Five dozen black ballpoints please.
JE: That's sixty black ballpoints.
CA: That's all, thank you.
JE: Right. Do you want to know the prices?
CA: No thanks. I'll wait for the invoice.
JE: OK. Now I need the official order. Can you send it as soon as possible please?
CA: I'm putting it in the post right now.
JE: Thank you. Goodbye.
CA: 'Bye.

Consolidation Unit A

(Big Ben strikes 2)

SUSAN: It's 2 o'clock exactly and time for 'Your News'. the radio programme for you. This is Susan Simple with the news headlines.

The President of the United States is having talks today with the Russian premier in Moscow. They are discussing peace plans.

At home, figures for this month show that the cost of living is rising at a rate of 10%. Wages are only rising at a rate of 7%.

British Airflight today announced the timetable of their new supersonic jet aeroplane, the Concourse. The plane takes off on its first scheduled flight to New York at 10 am tomorrow morning.

Some good news. The pound is up again against the dollar. One pound is now worth 2.26 US dollars.

Unemployment has reached its highest figure ever. There are now two million people out of work.

Mr Ron Smith of Woking is this year's 'Salesman of the Year'. More about that later in the programme.

And now a reminder that British Summer Time ends tonight at 3 am. Don't forget to put your clocks back one hour when you go to bed.

Finally, the weather. It is cloudy over most of Britain today with rain in Scotland. The temperature is about 13° Centigrade, that's 58° Fahrenheit.

That's the end of the news headlines. Over now to Woking to the home of 52-year-old Mr Ron Smith, the salesman of the year.

INTERVIEWER: Here we are in Ron Smith's home in Woking. Congratulations, Ron, on being 'Salesman of the Year'.
RON: Thank you very much, Brian.
INT: Is your family pleased with the news?
RON: Well, Brian, my wife's very pleased about the champagne and my son is looking forward to the stereo. It's coming tomorrow.
INT: That's right. Your prizes are a bottle of champagne and a stereo, aren't they? . . . Um, how far away is your firm?
RON: I work for Smiths which is just up the road. I walk to work. It only takes 5 minutes.
INT: I see. Now, your name's Smith and you work for Smiths Manufacturing Company. Is it a family firm?
RON: Oh no. I only work there. Smith is a very common name. There are about twenty people called Smith in our firm.
INT: Well thank you very much, Ron Smith. And now back to Susan in the studio.
SUSAN: Thank you Brian. And now for our car number spot. Listen carefully to today's six car numbers. The first person to phone in with the colour and make of one of the cars wins today's top single record. Here are the numbers: HNJ 630D, UVC 545M, VKM 420H, DAP 354S, URG 287V, and OYJ 861W. I'll say them once again. That's HNJ 630D, UVC 545M, VKM 420H, DAP 354S, URG 287V and OYJ 861W. Just ring 123 5050 and tell us the colour and make of one of those cars. That's 123 5050. You could win today's top single record – Mr Monday. And here it is to end our programme.

Tapescript

Unit Six

Exercise 89

WOMAN: Can I speak to the man please?
MAN: Which man?
W: The one I spoke to before.
M: There are a lot of men in the company. Can you describe him?
W: Well, he's got short hair.
M: All the men in the company have got short hair. Is it straight or curly?
W: Oh, straight, I think. And he's got dark hair.
M: And has he got a moustache?
W: Oh yes. And a beard.
M: A beard. Oh, I know who you want. Richard. Can you come over here for a moment please? Is this the man you want, Madam?
W: No. That's not him. *My* young man wears glasses.

Exercise 94

SIMON: Well, Anne, my lamb cutlets are delicious. How's your roast beef?
ANNE: The beef's lovely, but my chips are a bit cold. I wish I'd had mashed potatoes like you.
S: That's the trouble with going to a restaurant. You always want what the other person's having. When I saw your prawn cocktail, I was really sorry I'd chosen soup.
A: Well, that was lovely.
S: Would you like a dessert?
A: No. I don't think I could manage one. You go ahead though.
S: Yes. I think I will. The black forest gâteau looks good, but I think I'd like the apple pie. Would you like cheese and biscuits or coffee?
A: Coffee please. Black.
S: Right.
WAITER: Are you ready to order dessert sir?
S: Yes please. We'd like one apple pie and two coffees please.
W: Would you like black or white coffee?
S: One black and one with cream please.
A: Er . . . perhaps I will have cheese and biscuits after all, if that's all right, Simon?
S: Of course. . . . And one cheese and biscuits please.

Unit Seven

Exercise 111

My name's David Richards. That's R-I-C-H-A-R-D-S, Richards. I'm still at school, but I finish next month so I'm looking for a job. I want to work in an office. I can use a switchboard because my sister's a receptionist and she showed me what to do, but I haven't got any experience. My teachers think I'm a very good student, but I haven't done any examinations and I haven't got any qualifications. I can't type and I can't do shorthand.

My name's Carolyn Bennett. That's C-A-R-O-L-Y-N, Carolyn, Bennett. B-E-double N-E-double T. I'm at secretarial college and my typing and shorthand speeds are very good. I can't use a switchboard and I haven't got any experience of working in an office. I want an office job, but I don't want to work for a large firm.

I'm Lorraine Welder. That's spelt W-E-L-D-E-R. Lorraine Welder. I'm married and I've got two children. I worked in an office before I was married and now my children are growing up I want to go back to work. I can use a switchboard, but I can't take shorthand. I can type a bit.

Exercise 113

Oliver Howard is dictating a letter of recommendation to his secretary.

OLIVER: Take a letter please, Miss Leonard. It's a letter of recommendation for David Richards. He's applying for the job of filing clerk/person Friday with Milgrom & Co. The letter's to Mr D Milgrom, Milgrom and Co, 29 Glengall Road, London NW6 2EK. Right then . . .
Dear Mr Milgrom. Thank you for your letter of the second of November. I am very happy to give David Richards a reference for the job of filing clerk stroke person Friday. New paragraph. He is cheerful, pleasant and helpful in class and he is intelligent and also efficient in his work. I can certainly recommend him for the job. Yours sincerely, etc, etc . . .

Unit Eight

Exercise 122

ANNE: Can you tell me the way to BOS from the station?
SIMON: Well, come out of the station and go straight ahead. At the roundabout take the second exit. Then you're on the main road to the town centre. At the crossroads turn right. BOS is the tall white building on the left.
A: Thanks. And can you tell me the way to the post office from BOS please?
S: Yes. It's very easy. Come out of BOS and turn left. At the T-junction turn right. The post office is on the right. It's opposite the bank.
A: That's useful. Are there any shops near BOS?
S: Yes. There's a supermarket and a newsagent's. Come out of BOS and turn right. At the crossroads go straight ahead. The newsagent's is on the left. Then keep on to the T-junction and turn left and you'll see the supermarket on the left . . . Oh yes. In case you want to go out and enjoy yourself, there's a cinema on Fifth Avenue near the station.

Tapescript

Unit Nine

Exercise 136

The petty cash figures for October come under four headings: postage, travel, stationery and sundries (that's all the other things). The amounts spent were:

Postage: in the first week, four pounds ten pence; four pounds ten; in the second week, two pounds forty pence; third week, three pounds twenty pence; and in the fourth week, two pounds eighty pence.
The amounts spent on travel were: first week, one pound ninety-six pence; second week, one pound twenty pence; third week, two pounds thirty-four pence; fourth week, two pounds exactly.
Stationery: in the first week, seventy-nine pence only; second week, one pound seventeen pence; third week, one pound sixty pence; fourth week, one pound forty-four pence.
And finally, sundries: first week, six pounds sixty-eight pence; second week, three pounds eighty pence; third week, six pounds thirty-two pence; and the fourth week, eight pounds twenty pence.
Just to check those figures again, horizontally this time.
First week, postage, four pounds ten; travel, one pound ninety-six; stationery, seventy-nine pence; and sundries, six sixty-eight.
Second week: two pounds forty; one twenty; one seventeen; three eighty.
Third week: three pounds twenty, two thirty-four, one sixty; and six pounds thirty-two.
And finally, the fourth week: two eighty; two pounds; one forty-four; and eight pounds twenty.

Unit Ten

Exercise 149

My name's Lorraine Welder and I was born on the 18th of April 1953. I'm married with two children. I live in London and my telephone number is 01-673 9201. I went to two secondary schools. The first was York Grammar School in York. I went there from 1964 to 1969 and I took my GCE O levels there. I passed 5 O levels. Then I went to a sixth form college to do my A levels. It was Preston Park Sixth Form College in Preston, but I left in 1970. I didn't do my A levels. Instead I did a one-year secretarial course at Longford Secretarial College in Brighton and I got a diploma. I started work in 1971 when I was 18. I was secretary to the manager of a small transport firm called Chambers Trucks in Brighton. I worked there for a year and I earned £20 per week. Then I moved to London. I got a job as a receptionist for Buffalo Books in Baker Street. I worked there for three years. I got married in 1972. but I stayed at work until I had my first child in 1975.

My salary when I joined Buffalo Books was £1,560 and when I left it was £2,600. They gave me a very good reference when I left and I'm sure I can get references from Mr Chambers and from the secretarial college.

Consolidation Unit B

(Big Ben strikes 6)
Here is Susan Simple in the news studio with 'Your News'.

SUSAN: Good evening.
The minimum lending rate is going up by $1\frac{1}{2}$% from its present rate of 12% to $13\frac{1}{2}$%. The MLR affects other lending rates so we can expect them to rise too. There is good news for savers though. The interest rates are also going up.
The members of OPEC, the oil-producing countries, met last night to discuss oil prices. If oil prices rise, the cost of living in most industrial countries will also rise.
The workers at Jones Brothers Engineering Works went on strike yesterday. They are striking over pay. Our interviewer talked to some of the people at the works:

INT: Now you both work for Jones Brothers. Why are you on strike?
1ST WORKER: Our wages are very low.
2ND WORKER: Yes. Our pay is terrible. Our last pay rise was over 2 years ago.
1ST WORKER: The cost of living is going up all the time, but our pay never goes up.
(Back in the studio)
INT: Mr Jones. Your workers are on strike. Why is that?
JONES: They want more money.
INT: And are you going to pay them more money?
JONES: The management is thinking about the problem, but we haven't got a lot of money at the moment.
INT: I see. Thank you very much, Mr Jones.
SUSAN: Sir Alan Smith, the founder and managing director of Smiths Manufacturing Company Ltd. died late last night at his home in Surrey. He was 84. Sir Alan founded his company in 1925 and he worked in it all his working life. He retired fourteen years ago. There was a minute's silence at the factory at midday today.
Traffic news now. Over to our reporter on the spot.
REPORTER: Police are telling motorists not to drive through the centre of town if possible. There was a bad accident at the junction of Brazilian Way and Italian Grove. The junction is completely blocked. Road works in Denmark Hill are completely blocking this road between Egyptian Street and Brazilian Way. Can we also remind you that Egyptian Street is one-way running from east to west. Motorists who must drive through the centre of town should turn (. . .) at the roundabout in Italian Grove and use (. . .) and (. . .).

135

Tapescript

SUSAN: And now, let's take a look at the Financial Times share index over the last six months. At the beginning of the year the index was at 456.2, but it rose sharply in January to 474.5. It fell slightly in February by 5.2 points to 469.3 and then went up again in March to 473.9. In April it dropped sharply to 455.4. In May it rose by 10 points and in June it rose again slightly by 3.2 points. The Stock Exchange closed yesterday, the last day of June, at 468.6.

And finally, there was a bomb scare at a London store today. Mrs Ann Roach, who works at the store, went out to do some shopping in her lunch hour. She left her box of sandwiches under her desk in the corner of the office . . .

MAN'S VOICE: We apologise for losing Susan there. There is a small problem in the studio. Programmes will continue as soon as possible. In the meantime, here is some music.

Unit Eleven

Exercise 173

HOWARD: Good morning, Miss Bell. Before I ask you any questions, I'd like to go through your work record card . . . Now I see that you can do shorthand, but that you've never taken the minutes in a meeting before.

ANNE: That's right. My shorthand speeds are very good, but I haven't actually taken the minutes officially in a meeting. I'm sure I could soon learn though.

H: Quite. Now I'm sure you've used a photocopier before, but have you ever sent a telex?

A: No. I've done a lot of photocopying, but I've never used a telex machine.

H: Well, if you can use a typewriter and a telephone you shouldn't find it too difficult.

A: Oh yes. My typing speeds are very good and I can certainly use a telephone . . . in fact I can work a switchboard.

H: Well, I suppose that might come in useful. Now, have you ever typed reports before?

A: No, but I'm sure I can soon learn the layout of a report.

H: Uh-huh. Now, one of your jobs will be to order the stationery. Have you done that before?

A: Oh yes. In my first job I was in charge of ordering the stationery. On your form though you asked whether I've kept a petty cash book before. I'm afraid I haven't.

H: Oh well, perhaps that's one of the first things you should learn in your new job . . .

Exercise 178

We're quite proud of the new typewriter. The punctuation marks are much more clearly set out. In the top row, the asterisk is on the first key on the left. Next are the inverted commas. The oblique is on the third key from the left and the apostrophe is on the fourth key. On the far right at the top is the hyphen and the third and second keys from the right are the left and right-hand bracket signs. On the second row at the far right is the colon and to the left of that is the question mark. The semi-colon is on the third row below the colon. Below the semi-colon is the full stop. On the bottom row and to the left of the full stop is the comma. Of course to make an exclamation mark you have to use the full stop and the apostrophe.

Exercise 180

OLIVER HOWARD: Take a letter please, Miss Leonard. It's to Brighter Office Supplies Limited in Harlow. You can find their address in the newspaper advertisement. Right . . . Dear Sirs comma. New paragraph. I have seen your advertisement for office equipment in the Evening Star. Full stop. New paragraph. I would be grateful if . . .

MISS LEONARD: Excuse me, how do you spell grateful?

OLIVER: What? Mm. G-R-A-T-E-F-U-L. Grateful. Now where was I? . . . Yes . . . I would be grateful if you would send me your full catalogue and price list. Full stop. New paragraph. I look forward to hearing from you. Yours faithfully, comma, etc, etc. Would you read that back please?

MISS LEONARD: Dear Sirs. I have seen your advertisement for office equipment in the Evening Star. I would be grateful if you would send me your full catalogue and price list. I look forward to hearing from you. Yours faithfully.

OLIVER: That's fine. Type it up as soon as possible please.

Unit Twelve

Exercise 189

PENELOPE: I don't think it's fair. I work much harder than you do and you earn more than I do.

RICHARD: That's not true.

P: Yes it is. You earn £4,500 and I only earn £3,000.

R: Well yes, that's true . . . but I work a 40-hour week and you only work 35. If you want something really unfair, look at Susan. She earns £6,000 and she only works between 20 and 30 hours per week . . . and she has two months' holiday. I only have one.

P: Well, even that's longer than I have. I only have three weeks. You're right about Susan though.

R: And I've just remembered something else. She only had three months' training.

P: That's right. I did a six-month training course.

R: And I trained for a year. Anyway, it's probably because she's the eldest in the family.

P: Mmm . . . No. It's still not fair. You earn more than I do and I'm older than you.

Unit Thirteen

Exercise 201

Write down the answers to these simple calculations.

NO. 1: Two times three. (*6 – six*)
NO. 2: Eight divided by two. (*4 – four*)
NO. 3: Nine plus one. (*10 – ten*)
NO. 4: Seven minus four. (*3 – three*)
NO. 5: A hundred plus one. (*101 – a hundred and one*)
NO. 6: Ninety minus ten. (*80 – eighty*)
NO. 7: Eighteen divided by two. (*9 – nine*)
NO. 8: Six times three. (*18 – eighteen*)
NO. 9: Forty divided by four. (*10 – ten*)
NO. 10: Thirteen plus two. (*15 – fifteen*)

Exercise 202

SIMON: 'Morning George. I've got a complaint about a missing memo. I typed the memo to Fred McLean three days ago and it hasn't arrived yet. Have you seen it?

GEORGE: A memo to Fred McLean? I'm not sure. But I see a lot of memos and letters each day.

S: Yes, but . . .

G: Let me explain the system to you, then you'll understand . . . Every morning the postman delivers the post and it's sorted into two categories: business letters and personal or confidential letters. The business letters are opened and then all the mail is distributed to the different departments.

S: But that's nothing to do with my memo.

G: Wait a moment. I'm coming to your memo . . . Now, every afternoon all the post – including your memo – is collected from each department and sorted into four categories: internal post, first class letters, second class letters and parcels. The parcels are wrapped, labelled and weighed and the letters are weighed if necessary, that is if they look heavy. Then all the post is franked and taken to the postbox before half past five.

S: And the internal post? What happens to memos?

G: The internal post is distributed each morning with the incoming post.

S: That's very interesting, but it still . . .

G: Can I ask you a question, young man?

S: Yes, of course.

G: Did you put your memo in an envelope?

S: Er . . . maybe. I don't remember.

G: Did you put it in *this* envelope addressed to Fred McLean?

S: Yes. That's the one.

G: Hmmm. It was posted with the outgoing post. The postman has just returned it.

S: Oh no!

Unit Fourteen

Exercise 220

1

ANNE: Good morning. Sales department.
CALLER: Good morning. Can I speak to Sheila Baker please?
A: I'm afraid she isn't in the office at the moment. Can I take a message?
C: Yes. Can you tell her David Rogers phoned, of Rogers & Co. I want to speak to her about our order number 0804, but I'm leaving the office at about 5 o'clock.
A: Right. I'll ask her to ring before 5. Does she know your telephone number?
C: No. It's 854524. It's quite urgent.
A: I'll give her the message. Goodbye.
C: Goodbye.

2

A: Good morning. Sales department.
C: Good morning. Can I speak to Sheila Baker please?
A: I'm afraid she isn't in the office at the moment. Can I take a message?
C: Yes. Can you tell her Fiona Donaldson rang from Of-Op Ltd. I want to see her one day next week about some new office furniture.
A: Certainly. I'll ask her to ring you. Does she know your number?
C: She should do, but it's 59761.
A: I'll give her the message. Goodbye.
C: Goodbye.

3

A: Good morning. Sales department.
C: Good morning. Can I speak to Sheila Baker please?
A: I'm afraid she isn't in the office at the moment. Can I take a message?
C: No. It's all right. I'll ring again. It's not urgent. It's a personal call.
A: Can I tell her who rang?
C: Yes. Adam Haines.
A: I'll give her the message. Goodbye.
C: Goodbye.

Tapescript

Unit Fifteen

Exercise 227

SIMON: Take a good look at Harlow, Anne. Next year it's all going to be different.

ANNE: Oh is it? Why?

S: The planners are going to change it. At the moment they say there's too much traffic on Maddox Road, so they're going to make Rose Hill one way.

A: But the number eight bus goes along Maddox Road. Are they going to change that?

S: Yes. The bus goes the wrong way. The new bus route is going to start at the station, go down Fifth Avenue, straight across at the roundabout down Central Avenue, and then it's going to turn left at the next roundabout into Second Avenue and carry on along its old route.

A: Well, that's not really a very big change.

S: I haven't finished yet. They're going to close the station.

A: Close the station? Why?

S: Because not enough people use it. We've still got the other station in town.

A: How are you going to get to work?

S: I'll have to catch the bus from the other station. The number 10 goes right past BOS.

A: You're right. That's the one I get . . . What else are they going to do?

S: Well, the supermarket near the newsagent's is going to move to the roundabout near us. It's going to be on the corner between Fifth Avenue and Fourth Avenue.

A: That's a bit closer than the old one. Are they going to do anything to the bank or the post office?

S: No. They're staying where they are. There's something else you'll be pleased about though. They're going to open a new cinema right opposite BOS.

A: That's good. But what are they going to do with the old one?

S: Knock it down.

A: Oh well. That's progress I suppose. Is that all?

S: No. They're going to build a new roundabout at the junction of Fourth Avenue and Elizabeth Way.

A: And when's all this going to happen?

S: Well the planners say it's going to happen next year, but they haven't given us a date yet. In my opinion, it might never happen.

Consolidation Unit C

(Big Ben strikes 6)
Here is Susan Simple in the news studio with 'Your News'.

SUSAN: Good evening.

The workers at Whitaker's biscuit factory are on strike again. This is the second strike at Whitaker's this month. The strike is about pay.

An insurance company made a record profit last year, but the employees aren't going to get any of it. The FPA insurance company say that they have got other plans for the money. The employees are holding a meeting tonight.

The funeral of Sir Alan Smith, the managing director of Smiths Manufacturing Co Ltd, was held this afternoon at St Mary's church, Woking. Sir Alan leaves a wife, three children and two grand-daughters, the children of his second child. Sir Alan's elder son, who is unmarried, is taking over the company.

The temperature last night was minus 10° Centigrade. This is the lowest temperature ever recorded in London. The weathermen say it's going to be cold again tonight.

And finally, we're looking for reporters and newsreaders to work with us here in the newsroom. All you've got to do is to make a 10-minute news programme. We're offering a prize for the best programme and we will consider job applications from anyone who enters the competition. Listen to 'Your News' tomorrow at six for further details.

And that's the end of the news. From me and from all of us at the newsroom, goodnight.

List of irregular verbs

INFINITIVE	GERUND/ PRES. PARTICIPLE	PAST TENSE	PAST PARTICIPLE
be	being	was/were	been
bend	bending	bent	bent
break	breaking	broke	broken
burn	burning	burnt	burnt
buy	buying	bought	bought
catch	catching	caught	caught
come	coming	came	come
cost	costing	cost	cost
do	doing	did	done
draw	drawing	drew	drawn
dream	dreaming	dreamt	dreamt
drink	drinking	drank	drunk
drive	driving	drove	driven
eat	eating	ate	eaten
fall	falling	fell	fallen
feel	feeling	felt	felt
find	finding	found	found
forget	forgetting	forgot	forgotten
get	getting	got	got
give	giving	gave	given
go	going	went	gone/been*
have	having	had	had
hear	hearing	heard	heard
know	knowing	knew	known
learn	learning	learnt	learnt
leave	leaving	left	left
make	making	made	made
mean	meaning	meant	meant
meet	meeting	met	met
pay	paying	paid	paid
put	putting	put	put
read	reading	read	read
ride	riding	rode	ridden
ring	ringing	rang	rung
rise	rising	rose	risen
run	running	ran	run
say	saying	said	said
see	seeing	saw	seen
sell	selling	sold	sold
send	sending	sent	sent
sit	sitting	sat	sat
sleep	sleeping	slept	slept
speak	speaking	spoke	spoken
spend	spending	spent	spent
stand	standing	stood	stood
swim	swimming	swam	swum
take	taking	took	taken
teach	teaching	taught	taught
tear	tearing	tore	torn
tell	telling	told	told
think	thinking	thought	thought
understand	understanding	understood	understood
wake	waking	woke	woken
wear	wearing	wore	worn
win	winning	won	won
write	writing	wrote	written

* He has gone to America. = He is still there.
  He has been to America. = He has come back from America. He is not there now.

139

Longman Group U K Limited
Longman House, Burnt Mill, Harlow,
Essex CM20 2JE, England
and Associated Companies throughout the world

First published 1982

Fifteenth impression 1990

ISBN 0-582-51543-2

Produced by Longman Singapore Publishers Pte Ltd.
Printed in Singapore.

This book is dedicated to my father, isn't it?

Acknowledgements
The author wishes to acknowledge her debt to all those involved in the production of
this book, with special thanks to Michael Cass, David Cobb, Delia Greenall and
Howard Middle.

We are grateful to the following for permission to reproduce copyright material:
Guinness Superlatives Ltd. for an extract simplified from *Guinness Book of Records*.

Our thanks to Peter Lake for the photographs on pages 2 (top left and right, and
middle right), page 6, page 10 (1, 2 and 5), 100 and 101.
All other photographs were taken by the Longman Photographic Unit.

Illustrators: Tony Baskeyfield, Mervyn Caldwell, Tony Morris and Julian Smith.

Cover illustration by Steve Pickard.